LOVE

is the

AGENDA

L♥VE *is the* AGENDA

National Writer and Recording Artist

GREG BROWN

COVET & BEQUEST PUBLISHING

Library of Congress Cataloging-in-Publication Data is available upon request.

COVET & BEQUEST
PUBLISHING

Edited by: Sharman J. Monroe
Cover Photo by: Jonathan Keitt
Cover and Interior Design by: Jose Pepito Jr.

Published in the United States of America
ISBN: 979-8-9857305-1-7 Paperback
ISBN: 979-8-9857305-6-2 Hardback

"Enjoy life with your wife, whom you love, all the days of this meaningless life that God has given you under the sun."

– KING SOLOMON

CONTENTS

LOVE
is the
AGENDA

HAVE YOU EVER
BEEN IN LOVE?

*H*ave you ever been in love? Take a moment. Think about it. Have you ever been so blindly in love that the thought of the person you love being anything but perfect didn't exist? Can I ask you another question? Did someone come to mind? I will not ask you who, but I'm curious to know is it the person you're dating now, or is it the person you used to date? Is it the person you really wanted to be your husband? We'll keep that a secret for now.

> **Have you ever been so blindly in love that the thought of the person you love being anything but perfect didn't exist?**

It's okay. Don't tell me, but I'm sure you'll ponder on that question for a minute. Maybe you'll write me and tell me all about it.

May I ask you another question? Did your past love you thought was perfect eventually reveal itself as imperfect? Now you're here in the present, trying to make the best out of a new love and a new person, who secretly, isn't your number one draft pick. If only you could have remained blind to all the things you now hate about the person you used to be truly in love with. I probably shouldn't say hate. Hate is such an ugly word. But let's be honest, you did hate him towards the end. You hated him because he was causing your perfect love to end. The relationship you used to think was so perfect and you wanted everyone to see and believe you two had the perfect relationship is now over. You sit and think about all the wasted time taking and editing pictures for Instagram. Planning all the right Caribbean trips to post pictures of your happy relationship. Booking the best excursions, at the best resorts, with the best views, for your Instagram story. So much time spent ordering the perfect swimsuits for every day you spent with your former boo posing for pictures on the beach. All of that, so everyone felt like you and your former boo were the best couple ever. Now it's over.

So you erase every picture of him. Any incident or thing that makes you reminisce about him is gone. Okay, maybe not those shoes, and maybe not that bag. (lol!) But you still hated him. Why? Because he made you see all the bad things about him you never thought you'd see. It's his fault you're not blindly in love anymore. Isn't it crazy, with all the things you hated about him, he still comes to mind first? Before your current boyfriend, girlfriend, new crush, or the person your mom, dad, or friend tell you that you should be with. You thought about him first. The ex. The person you fought for years to get over. The person you're still trying to get over. The person you made yourself hate so you could stop thinking about him, missing him, and so you could stop crying and skipping meals because you couldn't get him off your mind. But you didn't. He's still there, tucked away, hidden from everyone, including yourself, until you have a moment. The person, who at the end of the relationship, you told everyone who asked about him only the bad things he did that hurt you. You did this to convince yourself and "your arena"—your circle of friends—that you weren't the problem, your ex was, and that's why you left him. His loss! Or was it?

I'm only asking that question because he came to mind first when I asked you, have you ever been in love? Maybe you'll never go back. Maybe everyone says you shouldn't go back. But if he came to mind, maybe your heart still wants to go back. Maybe a piece of you still has hope that one day, someplace, you two will bump into each other, and maybe he hasn't gotten over you either. We all think about those "what ifs." What if we kept trying? What if we went to counseling? What if he changed? What if I didn't listen to my arena? What if I kept listening to my heart? What if I didn't force myself to date other people? What if? I know you thought what you were doing would make you happy and it did. But it didn't make you happy the way he made you happy. And that's why you still think about him. Something is missing. You try to force yourself to love your new boo more, but something is still missing. Everything in the relationship is right, but there's still something off. We all know what that something is. Your friends ask how things are going with your new boo, and you smile and say, "I'm happy." You don't want them to think you're tripping. You know you have a good one, and you don't want them to think you're still thinking about your "sorry-a** ex." They helped you get out of that relationship. Let's be honest; some may have talked you out of the relationship. But, if you're happy now, why does it still feel like something is missing? You start to wonder if you just like "toxic-a** n*****," right? Could be both, but being happy and being fulfilled, are two different things.

Are you fulfilled? If so, why do you still think about your ex? Why do you try to act uninterested when his name comes up when deep inside you want to know? You want to know what he's doing? Did he move on? Does he have kids? How does his new boo look? Does he still think about you? Every day, you hope you don't log on and see a Facebook post displaying he got engaged. OMG! Can you imagine? Did your heart drop? Don't lie. I know you'd try to be politically correct and say you're happy for him. Maybe you'd even like the post. But deep down inside, you know you wouldn't be happy for him. I

> *Are you fulfilled? If so, why do you still think about your ex?*

know at some point, when no one was around, you'd look up his social media pages. I'm not judging you, but I'd bet his name is in your search history. We all might get in a little trouble if our significant other looked at our social media search history. (lol!) It's okay. We all do it. But just in case, clear your search history right now. (lol!) So again, I'll ask you. Have you ever been in love?

I'm only asking you this question because if you're in love now and the person you're with didn't come to mind first, is he your true love? Or are you blind? I'm trying to help you see that "true love" differs from being "in love." There are many examples of love. We love our favorite shoes until we buy a new pair. We miss our childhood dog that died until we get a new one, then Lassie's old news. What I'm saying is, even married people move on. We all know people who have been married one, two, and going on three times. We also know how much they were "in love" each time they got married. My point is, falling in love is easy. We fall in love, repeatedly. Well, most of us. Some of you hit the lottery with the first person you dated, and they became your true love for a lifetime. Kudos to the lucky ones! We all hate you so much! (lol!) But, for the rest of us losers who didn't meet our true

> *I'm only asking you this question because if you're in love now and the person you're with didn't come to mind first, is he your true love?*

love on the first try, I'll continue trying to explain the difference between in love and true love.

We all fall in love, break up, and fall in love, repeatedly. But we have one true love. At least, I think so. One person we can never shake the thought of no matter how many years have passed or how happy we are. No matter how many kids we have or how beautiful our wedding is, we still think about our true love—the ex. I know two women who were seconds away from walking down the aisle to be married and their grooms had no idea their soon-to-be wives were in tears, unsure if they were marrying the right man. How do I know? I may or may not have been the man one or both wanted to be their husband. (shrugs) They did marry their grooms, but I do not have to tell you how those marriages are going. See, it's not that they weren't in love with their fiancée. It's that their fiancée wasn't their true love. Although their minds may have made the logical decision, the heart wants what the heart wants. We call that "toxic" these days.

Anytime someone keeps going back to the same person, people call it toxic. They say you can do so much better. You should date so and so. You need to take some time for yourself. You're so stupid. I think we all have been told this before or said this to someone before. I read a few definitions of toxic, and these are a few of its meanings: poisonous, harsh, very harmful, and malicious. Some of you have been in toxic relationships, and I hope you left the relationship or you will leave the relationship immediately. I don't think I've dated anyone that fits that description. I haven't experienced those relationships, but my exes may beg to differ. I don't know. My relationships weren't perfect. Yes, we did have our crazy moments. I was a very damaged man, and I've dated some damaged women. One was admitted into a mental health facility a few times, but I wouldn't call her toxic. Toxic is a strong word that people label failed relationships nowadays. But I agree, some relationships are toxic.

Not only can intimate relationships be toxic, but also many other forms of relationships can be toxic. The relationship we have with God can be toxic at different points in our lives. As we all mature at different rates in human relationships, we also mature at different rates with our relationship with God. The difference is, God doesn't abandon us at our lowest moments or because we aren't doing what He wants us to do at a specific moment. God is closer to us at our lowest moments, and we are closer to Him when things are at their worst. He's patient with us throughout our lives. "In your relationships with one another, have the same mindset as Christ Jesus" (Philippians 2:5 NIV).

> *In human relationships, we distance ourselves when someone isn't doing what we want them to do or if they aren't acting how we want them to act.*

In human relationships, we distance ourselves when someone isn't doing what we want them to do or if they aren't acting how we want them to act. If they fail, we remind them or we make them make it up to us. I was the king of "make it up to me." That's one of the few charac-teristics of us master manipulators. I'll get into that later. Ironically, at the same time our partner is falling short in the relationship, we are usually falling short as well. With God, if we are failing in our relationship with Him, He doesn't listen to anyone telling Him to leave us alone or anyone telling Him to find someone new to love. But, Lord knows, that's the number one thing people are told to do and how to deal with relationships today.

> *Ironically, at the same time our partner is falling short in the relationship, we are usually falling short as well.*

Some of you have coun-sel, but you don't have good counsel. The Bible says, "Plans fail for lack of coun-sel, but with many advis-ers they succeed" (Proverbs 15:22 NIV). Just because your friend, mom, or dad may have an opinion on your life and relationships, it doesn't mean it's good counsel. I believe you should research and seek God first. Pray and ask God to lead you to the perfect counselor for you and your significant other.

I once read an excerpt from the book *New Day, New You* by Joyce Meyer. Mrs. Meyer said something I loved and think every person in a relationship with problems should do first. She said, "When you are in trouble, go to the throne before you go to the phone." You can't tell me a lot of you don't go to the phone first. A lot of you have an arena cheering you on when you do something good or something they like. Or your arena could be a circle of people tearing you down and booing you when you aren't doing something they like or something they enjoy. Your arena wants the best for you, but your arena doesn't own the team. You do! They're just fans.

Just like your favorite basketball team or football team has an arena full of people who support them when they're winning and boo them when they're losing, so do you. You're the Owner, General Manager, and Star Player of your team. Your boyfriend or girlfriend is your co-owner or teammate. Those are the only people who should have control of your team. NOT YOUR ARENA! You know who your arena is. It's usually your friend, co-worker, mom, dad, a book, TV shows, or you're comparing your team to another person's team in real life or on social media. It's okay to listen to those close to you. We all do. But let's be honest. Most of those people I listed above don't have their relationships or life in order either. If they do, how many years and how many mistakes did it take them to get there?

My point is, you must seek good counsel if you need help with your relationship. Good counsel may not be the people around you. The people around you may be biased, only seeing your side of the relationship. They may not have a true example of a winning relationship for you to mimic or follow. Just because

> *My point is, you must seek good counsel if you need help with your relationship.*

your girlfriend has experienced bad relationships or marriage that doesn't mean she can recognize the best relationship for you. You want your counsel to be someone or some people who reflect the relationship qualities you desire. Not some, and maybe not all, but a lot of the qualities you desire in your relationship. A good counselor will have the knowledge to understand and comprehend your relationship and the experience and know-how to help you get your relationship to where it needs to be in the future.

Most relationships these days are failing because they lack good counsel. Either the people in the relationship are trying to counsel themselves or too many opinions are influencing the relationship. The relationship doesn't have the right people helping the relationship succeed. Good counsel isn't necessarily her friends or his friends. Good counsel isn't biased. Most of you have counsel that's biased. That's not good counsel. That's the counsel you want in your lawyer. Your lawyer should be biased and working solely for you, not the other side. Good counsel should be bettering the relationship between you and your significant other.

Take a moment and reflect on your current counsel. This could be your friend, family, co-worker, or maybe an ex-lover. There are all types of counsel meddling in other people's relationships. Is your current counsel more so for you or your mate? Are they working for you both equally in the relationship? Be honest. I'd bet my entire closet they are solely, if not entirely, interested in bettering you and your desires. Hold on. Before I get too far, let me take a moment to say I'm not justifying, nor do I support abusive relationships. If you're in an abusive relationship that friends, family, co-workers, and others are telling you to end. I strongly agree. Domestic violence should not be tolerated. If you're in an abusive relationship, leave immediately and seek help. I'm also not telling you to stay in a relationship that isn't for you or that doesn't make you happy. I'm speaking to people who left a "true love" relationship for an "in love" relationship.

A lot of you have settled for the "seat filler." Do you know what a seat filler is? A seat filler occupies a spot until the person who the spot belongs to returns to his or her spot. A seat filler is someone in a spot because the person whose spot it is has left or isn't there for whatever reason. The seat filler is only there because the person who truly has your heart is no longer there. So you've chosen some poor unknowing sap to hold your true love's spot until he returns, or until you're finally over your ex and are ready to move on. In my relationship counselor's opinion, most of us need to take six months to a year to heal before moving on to someone else. Easier said than done, right?

> *A lot of you have settled for the "seat filler."*

Most of you settle for the unknowing and oblivious sap you make the seat filler instead of following your heart. I somewhat understand why some women settle. Men can be difficult. The more handsome, more athletic, more successful, more money, and most of all, the more street we are, the harder it is for you to break through to us. You're worn out by the time we're finally ready and finally understand the nagging wasn't nagging at all; it was ineffective communication. You were communicating, but we failed to comprehend or chose not to. We failed to be vulnerable with the woman we loved. Your communication was only ineffective because you were ready to take the next steps forward, and we weren't ready yet. By the time we are ready, you're broken, hurt, and too embarrassed to stay. You finally build the willpower to leave the man most of your friends and family have been begging you to leave for years. You build up a wall around your heart, and soon to follow are those famous words we all say to our soon-to-be-ex, "I tried to warn you that one day I was going to be completely done. I'm done! I don't want this anymore." Now he's begging you to stay, and you're in pain trying your best to walk away. I feel your pain. It took me years to finally see what we as men are doing to the women we love.

You may be asking yourself, *How did he finally see how horribly some men treat good women and push them to walk away?* In my past life, I was a huge drug trafficker, rapper with songs playing on your favorite radio station, and I enjoyed every woman who came along with the money, cars, clothes, and popularity. I was the n**** you hated you loved. I do think women are sometimes their own worst enemy, but I'll address that topic later. I finally understood where the gap in our relationships lies. I had to leave the streets. I had to retire from rap. I attended college and finished. I hired my own relationship counselor and went alone to help me figure out my flaws in my relationships. I had to stop looking in the mirror and only admiring the things on the outside. I had to look inside myself and identify all the flaws, bad habits, and ugly things that hurt, belittled, shamed, and broke people I said I loved. Looking inside is something many of us fail to do. It took me accepting responsibility and accountability for my f**ked up ways. Please forgive me for my vulgarity.

I am a spiritual man, and honestly, reading the Bible daily has helped me become the man I am today. But I'm still a work in progress. I'm far from perfect. I'm still growing and evolving. So, although I read and studied a lot of books on relationships from the genius minds of Michael A. Todd, Dr. Myles Munroe, Devon Franklin, Meagan Good, Dr. Sherri Keffer, Mira Kirshenbaum, Dr. Michelle R. Hannah, Joyce Meyer, Don Miguel Ruiz, Ian Kerner, Ph.D., and Gary Chapman about relationships to help me grow and understand how to be a better man in a relationship, I'm not them. I come from a different walk of life a lot of you can relate to. I'm writing from a different perspective.

I read those books to better understand how I've hurt women and how to earn forgiveness, love, and trust back from the people I hurt. I researched how to communicate with my companion, respect her, and most of all, how to control my sexual desires. I read books specifically for women to somewhat understand the damage I've done to women and understand how women heal and think. I did those things so I could better empathize with a woman's feelings and emotions. I respect the authors of the many books I've read! I've learned a lot, but I'm not a pastor or married yet. I'm speaking to you all from the mind of men who come from broken homes, strip clubs, hustling, womanizing, and overly ego-driven personalities. Yes, the mind of megalomaniacs, Machiavellianism, and sadistic men. I'm not afraid to say it, even if it pertains to me.

The first step to recovery is admittance. I'm speaking from the destructive mind of broken men who are egotistical, misogynistic, narcissistic, mentally abusive, and manipulative to the women and people they love. Men who have baby momma drama and too many friends buried in the ground or locked up in the federal penitentiary. I'm your professional athlete, entertainer, and D-Boy. I'm your arrogant corporate professional boyfriend who thinks he's better than you. I'm the man who thinks I'm the catch, not you, all while dressed in a suit. I'm explaining this to you so you understand that I will help you understand your mate, past mate, or sex mate better. I know we are confusing. I know we are broken men who built up a wall of ego and pride because we thought it would protect us from being vulnerable and getting hurt. I know the man we portray isn't the man you need or the man we truly are. "Do not consider his appearance or his height, for I have rejected him. The Lord does not look at the things people look at. People look at the outward appearance, but the Lord looks at the heart" (1 Samuel 16:7 NIV).

My life coach and relationship counselor, Dr. Michelle R. Hannah, always tells me, "Your ego is nothing but your imposter." A lot of us create a character and believe the image we've created is real. People do this online every day. A lot of us have created an avatar, character, and image of only the things we want people to see and believe about us in real life. I'm saying this to help you close the gap. I want you to see your mistakes. I want men to see their mistakes. Men, I want us to get help with our post-traumatic stress syndrome (PTSD) from our broken childhoods. I'm trying to break the curse. I want us to break the curse. I want loving functional relationships to be at an all-time high. I want you to believe in true love again.

> *"Your ego is nothing but your imposter."*

Men, we are f**king up! Women, you are too. The scales are broken. The balance is gone. Trust is pretty much extinct. As the Bible says, "You are not to do as we do here today, everyone doing as they see fit" (Deuteronomy 12:8 NIV). The word "love" is tossed around so loosely these days. Love used to mean everything to us. Love used to wake us up in the morning and talk us to sleep at night. Now love comes with amendments. If love is supposed to be unconditional, why do we have so many d*mn conditions in our relationship? Women, you all are running from one relationship to another. Men, you forgot we wanted to be husbands to our wives and fathers to our children as little boys, not dope boys, whores, and liars. We got money and sex, and forgot our dream. Women became objects for us to gain. And, women, you allowed yourself to become objects for us to gain in exchange for materialistic things, trips, and status quo. Status quo, meaning my man is better than yours! Ladies, is what you're gaining worth what you're losing? I'll get back to that.

Let me get back to my point about the man I am and used to be, and the type of man you love now or used to love. I'm not talking about squares or men you can run over, or men who do whatever you say. I'm not talking about men who are just happy they have a woman like you or finally got you. They knew you were out of their league and so did you. But you were tired, beat, and just wanted someone around to put up the blinds, wash the car, and take out the trash. Lord knows you were tired of taking out that trash, girl! (lol!) You wanted someone you could count on to attend your company's annual Christmas party. Someone you didn't have to worry about another woman telling you she's f**king your man. Someone you could trust, even though deep down inside, you know he isn't your true love. Some of you fell in love with a man who let you be the man of the house, and eventually, you resented him.

You resent him because he's not the Alpha Male you want. A man who is the perfect combination of street and corporate, or maybe he's just corporate, but he's no punk either. You want a man who can put on a suit or a pair of Timberland boots. You want a man you feel safe with any time and any place. A man you know, if things get rough, he will make a way. He's going to make sure you and your kids are okay no matter what. I'm talking about the man you really want. A real man! The man you love. The man who came to mind first when I asked you, "Have you ever been in love?" Yes, him. Your true love. The man you grew to hate. The man you said you'd never date again or anyone like him. But you always go back to him or you're attracted to men like him. After you reach the age of thirty to thirty-five years old, you try to date differently.

You may settle for a man who is the complete opposite of the man who has your heart. That's okay. But that's why you have that feeling something is missing in your relationship. That void. That's because no matter how much you love or like this guy, you know he's the seat filler. He'd better hope and pray you don't meet someone else or your ex doesn't come back around because his a** is grass. He's convenient. He's the safe-zone-mate.

> *You may settle for a man who is the complete opposite of the man who has your heart.*

You all know the safe-zone-mate, a.k.a. seat filler. White women, black women, brown women, and yellow women know all about the safe-zone-mate. He's who you dated to avoid being hurt, again. Unfortunately, you're still hurting, sweetheart. You've just learned to mask the hurt. Your safe-zone-mate doesn't know why you're distant at times. He doesn't understand why everything he does right is always wrong to you. He doesn't understand why you shut him out. He doesn't understand why at times you feel so distant.

He doesn't know he's only there to fill in the blank. On the outside, everything seems perfect. But on the inside, you both know something isn't right. But you both keep moving along, hoping the feelings will change and things will get better. They won't. You may stay together for the kids or to keep up the appearance of the wholesome couple. You may come to a point you give up, stay, and say it is what it is, and that's okay.

I'm not judging you. You're older now and this is comfortable for you. You don't want to date again or try things again with your ex, so you've chosen to be "happy," but you're not fulfilled. As bad as the relationship with your ex seemed or was portrayed to be, you were fulfilled when you were with him. If only he would have been around as much the seat filler you replaced him with. You were only unhappy when he wasn't around and out doing God knows what. You only nagged him because you wanted him to stop and see you were a good woman, and he'd better not mess this up! You told him if he keeps it up, one day, he will lose you, and you're never coming back! Well, he messed up, and you left, and now you're sticking to your word of never coming back. Are you happy? Are you fulfilled? Could something else have been done to help maintain and fix the problems in your relationship? I think so.

Don't get me wrong. Some of your relationships needed to end. Forever? I don't know. But some of your relationships did need to end permanently. Let's be honest. You were trying to put out a California brush fire with a Nerf water gun.

Never going to happen. But I do think 80-90% of true love relationships are salvageable. Before dating apps, bachelorette TV shows, *Real Housewives*, who are majority divorced, and the social media era, for centuries, most couples stayed together and stayed married until death did them part.

Listen for a moment. Let me break something down about Greg. That's me, by the way. I'm a man. I'm a man's man. I'm a God-fearing man. I'm a father of a daughter. I'm a brother to sisters. I'm a son to a mother. God allowed me to mature without abandoning me or listening to someone telling Him to leave me alone and move on. "The steadfast love of the Lord never ceases; his mercies never come to an end." (Lamentations 3:22 ESV).

I was a "real n****." I used to tell my ex in any disagreement, "I'm a n**** first!" I was telling her, take it or leave it. My shortcomings and ignorance would not change because I am who I am and I didn't plan on changing. I was the man or n**** most of you dated or date. I was in the streets, and into you, probably into a couple of you, if you catch my drift. I'm the guy you were waiting on to mature. The guy you were waiting on to grow up. The guy you wanted to be the reason he gave up the street life and all of his other hos because he was madly in love with you. The guy you prayed for God to change and make him want the same things you wanted in your relationship.

The problem is, he had to learn how to love himself first. He wanted you to wait around. He didn't want to lose you. Unfortunately, he didn't have it in himself yet to be vulnerable enough to tell you he was weak. Not weak in the sense he wouldn't kill for you, his ego, or his friends. But weak because he wasn't ready for the things you wanted and deserved in the relationship. He was too selfish to tell you because he didn't want to lose you either. He wanted to spend the rest of his life with you, but he couldn't be a man and a real n**** at the same time, and he didn't know. He still may not know. He was unaware he didn't love himself. He thought he loved himself because he spoiled himself with women, cars, and clothes. So he hurt you, and as much as he knew it was causing him to lose you. He didn't want to let you go. In his mind, one day, he would get rich from selling drugs, music, or his new job, and he could fix everything he did wrong and make it up to you. He didn't realize by the time he got rich, you'd hate him. And you'd have so much hate and resentment built up in your heart you'd want to forgive him, but there were just too many scars on your heart, still bleeding, to forgive and forget all the f**ked up things he did to you. Too many things that still hurt you. Too much time you feel you lost.

Now, you're mad at yourself because you feel you didn't love yourself enough to leave. Now, a part of you doesn't forgive yourself for being so stupid! But you had hope. You hoped God heard your prayers, and miraculously, made your mate change one

> **You hoped God heard your prayers, and miraculously, made your mate change one day.**

day. Do you remember playing Tug of War as a kid? That's what your relationship was or is. It started off fun, smiles and laughs as one person attempted to pull the other person over to their side. We all think our side is better. At the same time, the other person feels their side is better, too. Then one side begins to lose and the winning side is happy. The loser is struggling and glimpses of smiles become strains and frowns. The loser gets pulled closer to the middle, but they never reach the other side. They fall into a hole. The winner doesn't really win either. The loser lets go, and the winner falls backward and gets dirty and hurt too. We play this game repeatedly until someone calls it toxic or says, "You're stupid for playing those games with him. You should have been left. A relationship shouldn't be that hard."

People say many things while spectating your relationship. I agree. Love shouldn't be a game of Tug of War. Someone should've come over and told you both to put down the rope. Step away from the hole. Let's discuss what both of you want, find a medium, and stop playing the game. True love exists. A lot of us lose it because we don't know how to maintain it. We want it our way. We involve too many people in our relationship during the honeymoon phase, so when the bad moments happen, we've invited too many outside opinions into our arena, and now we can't get rid of them. We have to keep face. We can't look stupid. We have to move on to someone who looks good to everyone and hopefully makes us "happy." Then that fades, and we do it all over again.

Love is not a pair of shoes you wear until they're no longer new and you get a new pair. Truth is, even some new shoes hurt. In love may be easy, but true love takes work. In love, you get over. True love, you'll never forget how he made you feel. Even with all the bad times, you can still feel him when you think of the good times. His face still pops up in memory when you pass a certain street, hear a certain song, smell a certain scent, or turn to his favorite TV show or movie. You remember his favorite food. You probably have a keepsake box put up somewhere full of all the memories you two shared, just in case you get back together and get married. You still think about him when you're with the seat filler. You wish the seat filler had some of his good qualities.

> *Love is not a pair of shoes you wear until they're no longer new and you get a new pair.*

Can I tell you a quick story? I lost a dear friend to murder. Despite the countless amounts of murdered friends I've experienced in my life, it never gets easy, especially losing him. We were close and very similar, both good and bad. We would always talk and share our plans, deepest thoughts and feelings about life, the streets, our kids, and most of all, the women we loved. I knew how much he loved and missed his ex despite his missteps and failures throughout their relationship. We both failed in very similar ways in our relationships.

Aside from the painful emotions that surrounded his sudden passing, the thing I remember most about his funeral was the words his ex shared with me while bearing a face full of tears after his funeral service ended. He and his ex had been together for over ten years before they split up. I knew she had moved on to be with someone else, but as I hugged and listened to her speaking in tears, she said, "Bettie, my heart is broken. I don't know what I'm going to do! I thought we had more time! I thought at some point we would end up back together. Now he's gone. What am I going to do? He is the love of my life. He is gone, Bettie! I don't know what I am going to do. I love that man. He is my heart!"

As I stood there in pain, disbelief, and hurt watching them lower my friend into the ground listening to her words and feeling the passion and pain in her voice, I was hurt even more. I knew how much he loved her. I knew how much he missed her. I knew how much he was changing his life to be a better man, father, and partner. I knew all the feelings she was sharing with me, he felt as well. Despite how happy, in love, and "kept" she was with her new man, at that moment, she realized her true love and soul mate was gone forever, and she had missed her opportunity to work things out with him. I believe she finally realized their pasts didn't matter, only their present. At that moment, she knew she was going home to her seat filler, and she would never have a chance in life to love, forgive, grow old, and *be present* with her true love, again. She was empty, she was defeated, and there was nothing she or anyone else could do about it.

Listen to me. True love requires you to slow down. It requires compromise. It requires good counsel to get past the miscommunications and disagreements. True love, you regret. In love, you regret you dated him at all. We all have a friend that falls in love every three months. We all have a friend who dates, but we all know she's still heartbroken over her ex, and it's been years.

Our great grandparents didn't have phones, a club on every corner, friends over in their business, and they didn't have LinkedIn, Facebook, Instagram, Snapchat, Pornhub, and dating apps influencing their thoughts and relationship status.

> ***True loves keep falling in love repeatedly with each other.***

They had to figure it out with God and love. Marriages that last forty and fifty years involve two people in true love, falling in and out of love, repeatedly, with each other. Do you see the part you missed? True loves keep falling in love repeatedly with each other. Love is work. It isn't always a picnic. I do believe in time, and over time, it becomes easier. In this day and age, to maintain a healthy relationship, you need good counsel. Perhaps you need to seek a professional counselor or a spiritual counselor. Someone to help you get through the bad moments and someone to help you get through the difficult times when you want to leave. Someone to help you communicate effectively when communicating with one another gets tough. Someone with a proven track record in their relationship and someone with a proven track record of relationship testimonies from people they've helped heal. Your relationship requires counsel from someone with the qualities in their relationship that you are looking to gain and achieve in your own relationship.

With so many distractions that exist in life and online, relationships are tough. There are so many distractions from home to work, we need someone to help us pull it all together when things are falling apart. We need someone to help us grow when things are stagnant. We need someone who can help us see how our childhood issues and personal flaws may be hindering our grown-up relationships. Had I sought counseling in any of my past relationships, they would have lasted far longer than they did, maybe even 'til death did us part. Unfortunately, we had the same counsel most of you use—friends and family. The common result of that type of counsel is failure.

I'm not telling you to force a relationship with someone you're not truly in love with or to go back to your ex. Maybe the perspective I'm sharing with you is for your next relationship. I want you to grow old with your true love, not with your seat filler. This chapter was written to help you see some of the stages relationships go through, ill-assisted and unassisted, that cause them to fail. Most people in relationships don't seek professional counseling until it's too late. A relationship with God and good counsel can result in maintaining a fulfilling relationship. Maintaining a relationship with your true love is the ultimate goal instead of settling for a relationship with someone you kinda love, don't love, grew to love, forced your-self to love, or may not be in *true* love with.

Imagine a relationship where both partners learn about themselves, their good and bad qualities, and work on those qualities positively, together. Imagine a relationship where both partners learn the best and most effective way to love one another without distractions and biased opinions. We'd see more people remaining faithful, loving each other uncon-ditionally, and staying in "true love" relationships, 'til death do them part. The ultimate nirvana.

IS THIS LIFE?

*I*s this life? Is this really what you've been looking forward to? Loneliness? Insecurity? Depression? Uncertainty? Your aunts asking you at every family gathering, when are you going to give them a baby? Strangers asking are you married? Your mother asking you, for the millionth time, when are you going to have kids? Until, one day, she stops asking you to avoid that recurring argument that ends with, "I don't know!" And you have to watch women you thought you were so much prettier than getting engaged and married. This can't be life!

Now look at you. Buying your own costume ring to wear on your wedding finger to avoid that infamous question, "Why aren't you married yet?" You say the ring is to stop men from talking to you, but we all know the reasoning behind that ring. That ring is to stop co-workers and strangers who think, "You're so pretty," from asking, "Why aren't you married?" Truthfully, has a wedding ring ever stopped a man from asking a woman is she happy and can he have her number? I don't think so.

Nowadays, men will ask you for your Instagram name to avoid asking you for your phone number and being rejected. We all want another social media follower, right? Oh, and I can't forget the most infamous pickup line of them all, "Your man doesn't let you have friends?" I'm sure you've heard that one before. So, let's be honest. A ring, or decoy ring, will not stop a man from asking you for your number. But this isn't how you expected your life to pan out, right? You were supposed to be married or at least engaged by the age of twenty-four. You were supposed to have the big house and one or two kids before you turned thirty. Some of you aren't twenty-four yet, or you just passed it, so you still feel confident.

Let me ask the confident women a question. Are you with Mr. "I Want To Spend The Rest Of My Life With You"? I doubt it. You may have kids, but have you met the man you want to spend the rest of your life with? I'm not talking about good d*ck or a rebound love. I'm not talking about the man you like. I'm not talking about someone you're in love with, but still unsure if he's husband

> *Are you with Mr. "I Want To Spend The Rest Of My Life With You"?*

material. I'm not talking about the seat filler. Maybe a few of you have met your soul mate. If you're still with him or not, I don't know. Thirty-year-old and over women, with your careers where you want them to be, are you with Mr. "I Want To Spend The Rest Of My Life With You"?

I'm sure your skin is poppin' and your hair is healthy, so what's the problem? I'm sure you've asked yourself many times, "Is it me?" I'm sure you've looked at girls you think you're better than and asked, how is she married and I'm not? How does she have the big house, kids, and a husband, and I don't? You ask yourself, *What am I doing wrong? Why am I out with my single or cheating girlfriends on a Saturday night, and she's at home posting the life I should be living? Why do my weekend plans only consist of going to Target, opening a bottle of wine, putting on nightclothes, and sitting in my bonnet watching reality TV?* You're home alone, skimming through Instagram and Facebook, comparing your life to people you probably don't know, while reading memes you believe were written just for you. Let's not forget to mention all the shopping you do for things you don't need, to attend places you don't have a husband to go with. Is this your life? No, really. Is this your life? Is this where you planned to be at this age and stage of your life? I'm serious. Was this the plan?

I know we like to blame everyone else for our shortcomings, but it can't be entirely their fault, right? You get down some days, but on good days you stand in your mirror looking cute and tell yourself you're pretty, a great catch, you have a good job, dudes try to talk to you all the time and your a** is getting fat. You tell yourself I don't care what anybody says, "I'm a catch and I don't need no man!" Ha! The lies you tell.

We try to convince ourselves that we don't need the things we really want when they seem unobtainable. Some of you have made God your man. Some of you have made online shopping your man. Some of you have made your mom your man. Uh oh! Did I touch a nerve? Yes, mom has become, for some of you ladies, your boyfriend. The relationship you should be growing with your mate at thirty years old, you're growing with your mom. You and mom talk, text, ping, and Facebook all day. You two plan spa days, trips, and travel together. She's become closer to you at thirty to forty than she's been to you all of your life. Mom has become more of your companion than the man in your life or the man you wish was in your life. (side-eye) Trust me; I get it. For most of us growing up, mom was all we had. She was our first love, our first friend, our first everything.

Good old reliable mom! Deep down inside, she wants you to be happy, have kids, and meet a good man. Her motives are pure, and so are yours, but let's be honest. Your excessive relationship as a grown woman with your mom only works for single women who want to remain single. If you have a man, and this is the dynamics of you and your mother's relationship, you'll probably be single soon. If this is the dynamics of you and your mother's relationship and he's okay with it, he either works a demanding job and his time is limited with you, so mom's presence works. Or, he's probably cheating and doesn't care how much time you spend with your mom, as long as he has time to go cheat.

Women in happy relationships don't have the inordinate time you have to hang with their sixty-year-old mother. To be honest, most women don't want to hang with their sixty-year-old mother all of the time. As children, we know we may have to take care of our parents at some point, but this is different. Some of you date based on your parents' opinions and approval. That's okay. We all listen to our parents, but some of you have made your parents your man, friend, kids,

> *You're filling the voids in your life with your parent(s) and that type of relationship can be unhealthy for the relationship you have or will have with your mate.*

and counselor. You're filling the voids in your life with your parent(s) and that type of relationship can be unhealthy for the relationship you have or will have with your mate.

From the beginning of time, humans grew up, left home, got married, had children, and mom and dad become weekend visits. We may call and check on them once a day, but they have a life, and so do we. Don't get me wrong. Men love your mom. We do, I promise. Men just don't want to date your mom. At some point, we all have to ask ourselves, why do I have this person so engulfed in my life? Why do they have so much to say about my life? Again,

I'm not picking on your mom. Don't beat me up. (lol!) *I love your momma.* I have a mom who wants the best for my life too. My mother wants the best for my sisters' lives as well. But she has her own life. She lives every day doing the things she loves, and that doesn't always include her daughters. Typically, her plans include her man. I'm only mentioning this because many men have issues with their girlfriend's mother influencing their girlfriend's decisions.

> **You should be communicating with your man.**

Some of you have had issues with your man's mother, so you understand what I'm saying. You know your mate, and you know when your mate is being influenced and his actions are different. I will be honest. Most of our parents have been single, married, and divorced. They have been in their own dysfunctional relationships. Some are still in those dysfunctional relationships. Instead of getting help, they hang out with you, when in actuality, they need to focus on their own relationship situation and bettering their own lives. Some have given up on life because it isn't going as planned, just like you are doing, so you both use each other as a crutch. This helps you both avoid dealing with the voids and unfortunate circumstances surrounding your lives.

Don't take what I'm saying offensively. It's okay to be close with your mother and your father. But the time you're communicating with your parents about your relationship, you should be communicating with your man. Don't tell your parents you're fed up, tired, planning to leave, or cheat. Tell your man. Be 100% transparent. The truth may hurt, but it's better than a lie. Yes, omitting any specific information is a lie. You wouldn't want to find out your man is planning to move on, or has moved on, after the fact. Be the noble person you'd want your man to be.

If you're in a relationship and you want the relationship to succeed, use the time you usually spend with your mother to plan spa days and vacations with your man. If you aren't in a relationship, work on yourself. Reflect on the setbacks you may have contributed to your past relationships. Cutting the cord will relieve some of the pressure and influence mom and dad have on your life. Yes, I said cutting the cord. When you were born, your parents cut the cord, but there was still an invisible cord your parents left attached to you until you got a little older and more independent. Some of you rebelled early and cut the cord yourself. The cord usually remains detached as you become a young adult. But for some of you, loneliness and uncertainty make you reattach the cord to mommy and daddy. "Mommy, I need you!" And here comes mommy to the rescue. Well, you two seem to think so. Your life isn't perfect. You may be single and lonely, but that doesn't mean you have to marry your mom. For some of you, your cash-back credit card has become retail therapy because being an adult is kicking your butt!

God may be blessing you with this time alone to grow, to engage in self-love and self-care, and to reflect on your good and bad habits. Maybe, like Jesus, this is your forty days and forty nights in the Judaean desert to fight off the temptations you're currently failing at. Or, maybe, like Moses, this is your forty days and forty nights on Mount Sinai to receive the commandments God has for you. The trials in your life you are trying to avoid may be a blessing from God you're blocking. The Bible says, "My child, don't make light of the Lord's discipline, and don't give up when he corrects you. For the Lord disciplines those he loves, and he punishes each one he accepts as his child" (Hebrews 12:5-6 NLT).

It's okay if life isn't going as planned. I doubt life is going as planned for anyone on earth. You're not the only person asking these questions. You're not the only person in bed by 8 p.m. on a Friday night. We're all trying to figure life out day by day, failing forward. A pastor I respect and know, Rev. Dr. Casey R. Kimbrough, told a story one Sunday about a peasant man who an angel visited:

> *It's okay if life isn't going as planned.*

> "The angel came to the peasant man and told him that God is going to bless him. God promised to bless him like a child of Abraham."

If you don't know about Abraham and how he and his entire bloodline were blessed, take a minute and open up your Bible to the book of Genesis. Okay, let me get back to the story.

"Then the angel told the man there was only one catch to God blessing him. The angel told the man God is going to give you whatever you ask for, but whatever you ask for, God is going to give your neighbor double of whatever He gave you. He thought about it for a minute, and then he happily accepted God's terms."

I mean, who would turn down a blessing from God? I wouldn't!

"So, the peasant man immediately made his first request. He asked God to give him a thousand cattle! Lo and behold, later that day, he looked outside and there they were! One thousand cattle gathered and walking around as far as his eyes could see. With that one act, God had lifted the man up from poverty. He was no longer a peasant man. The man was so happy that he praised God immediately!

The following morning the man looked out of his window, and guess what he saw? He saw his neighbor had two thousand cattle! Immediately, his praises to God for his one thousand cattle stopped. Then he remembered he had two more requests he could ask of God. So he immediately prayed and asked God for a son. He told God, 'I want an heir! I want a son blessed from God to inherit the wealth I have been blessed with.' So, he went into his bedroom with his wife, and nine months later, a son was born. He was so excited! He immediately gave God praise! He was elated and thanked God with all his heart! He immediately took his son down to the temple and told the priest, 'Look at my son! Look at how God has blessed us! We are so blessed! God is so good! Praise GOD!'

Then the man turned around, and in mid-sentence, he saw his neighbor. His neighbor said, 'We have been blessed too! We have been blessed with two sons!' And his neighbor praised God too! Immediately the man God blessed with one son stopped praising God. He looked frustrated, and he didn't look happy about his son or his neighbor's sons. Even though he had been blessed out of poverty into wealth by God and given a son, he wasn't happy. So he went home and prayed again. He said, 'God, I know what I want now! I want you to gouge out my right eye. Take my right eye, God!' When he made that request, the angel returned to his home. The angel asked him, 'Why would you request to have your eye gouged out? Why would you want your neighbor to be blind and unable to attend to his cattle or watch his sons grow up?' Then the angel told the man, 'God would not honor your request! God is a God of grace and mercy.'"

You see, we seem to lose sight of our blessings and God's mercy at times. We also fail to offer other people mercy and grace. I told you this story because if you don't feel like life is going right for you, it's probably because you're looking at someone else's life. You're envious of someone else's blessing. You're not giving them the same grace and mercy you want God to give you. You're comparing their life to yours and you don't understand why God is blessing them with double and triple right now, but not you.

> *If you don't feel like life is going right for you, it's probably because you're looking at someone else's life.*

The problem is you don't know what they've been through before God blessed them. Everyone's life and blessings are different. They come at different times. The scripture says, "You shall not covet your neighbor's wife. You shall not set your desire on your neighbor's house or land, his male or female servant, his ox or donkey, or anything that belongs to your neighbor" (Deuteronomy 5:21 NIV).

Let's be honest. Some people you're jealous of did not get their "blessings" from God at all. You have to stay focused on your race. I tell my daughter this quite often. Stay focused on your life and bettering yourself. Don't focus on your friends or social media. Keep your blinders on.

If you've ever watched or been to the Kentucky Derby, the horses racing have blinders on the sides of their eyes. They put blinders on the horses so they can't be distracted and stay focused. The horses don't need to focus on what their neighbors are doing. They should be focused only on their race. The Bible teaches us to focus on *our* own race. "Therefore, since we are surrounded by such a huge crowd of witnesses to the life of faith, let us strip off every weight that slows us down, especially the sin that so easily trips us up. And let us run with endurance the race God has set before us" (Hebrews 12:1 NLT).

> **There is no competition in your life!**

There is no competition in your life! God is blessing you too. The only reason you can't see it is because you're comparing your life to celebrities, friends, and social media pages you follow. The only reason you can't see it is because your single sixty-year-old aunt keeps asking you why haven't you had a baby yet? You can't see it because you got sick of being the bridesmaid, but not a bride somewhere along the line. Did you forget you have God, a job, home, friends, family, too many clothes, and a fatty? You're taking this time to better yourself mentally, spiritually, and emotionally, but most importantly, to avoid unnecessary mileage and body counts. That way, when God blesses you with Mr. "I Want To Spend The Rest Of My Life With You," you're ready!

Sometimes we can miss our own blessings because we are too busy counting someone else's blessings. I know, when I started off, you didn't know where I was going with this, but let me tell you! I want you to win! I want you to feel like love will conquer all again. I want men and women to slow down the sex, speed up the healing, and stop the dysfunctional relationship cycles.

It's okay to be single. Use that time to grow your relationship with God, study yoga, travel, learn a new language, get a degree, or start your own business. Don't date because you're lonely. Don't add a new body or three to your sexual encounters every year. If momma needs to work on herself, tell her she needs to work on herself, too. If she's married and having problems in her marriage, tell her she needs to work on things with dad so she can spend all the time she's spending with you, with him, without you! (lol!) Tell her she will see you soon enough when you're walking down the aisle or dropping off her grandkids so you and your husband can have a spa day, travel, or drink that bottle of wine you bought from Target.

> ### It's okay to be single.

Seriously, I want to help break all the curses that exist for us as men, women, and couples. A lot of us are products of generational curses that consist of broken homes, broken relationships, poor communication, infidelity, abuse, and abandonment. I want us to believe in marriage again. I want us to trust, again. Trust me; I'm no saint. I was the man who didn't want to marry you and I was the man you'd better not trust. But I'm also living proof that men can change. Men can grow up. Men do eventually mature.

At the beginning, somewhere I said, "Is this life?" Now repeat after me:

> "Yes. This is life. This is my life. I have the power to control my thoughts. This is the life God has chosen for me. I will focus on the message and not the mess. I will be the blessing and no longer the curse. I am everything I need to be and more. I will cease every negative thought and cast them over to God. I will only focus on the positive parts of my life. Things may get bad, but they will get better. Someone had plans for tomorrow, but they will not live past today. So I will focus on my today. Today, I am here and I am blessed.
>
> Today, I realized God blessed me with yesterday and today. Amen."

Look at God! I think I also asked, "Is this really what I was looking forward to?" No. Not all of it. Who looks forward to a bad day or a bad anything? But you learn from that lesson and maybe one day, that lesson can be a blessing of wisdom for someone else who needs to be lifted. See, that's grace. We may not have everything we want in life, but I believe that's how God intended it. If we had everything, what would we have to look forward to? God doesn't give us all of our smiles at once. He gives us our smiles spread out across our entire life at different moments. Some are big and some are small, but those smiles keep us going! I believe when we are just about at our wit's end and ready to give up, the love of our life will walk right in and give us that big smile God always planned to give us when the time was right. Maybe he's already there. Maybe you've been thinking about calling him. I don't know. But I do know that you know. If there is someone you know is the love of your life, what are you waiting for? Call him! If there's someone already there, and deep inside, you know he shouldn't be there, end it. Quit playing with fate. If you don't want it, let it go. If you do want it, hold on to it and never let it go. Get focused on growing yourself and healing. If he is there and is the love of your life, and you're playing around, get focused. Tell momma you will talk to her later because you and your mate are making a plan, clarifying it, and agreeing to secure a future together.

I understand, sometimes it's hard to get the other person on the same page. That's okay. Research and call a good counselor today. He may not want to go, but if he loves you and he wants things to grow and work, he will eventually go. Trust me. I've been the person who refused to go, and I've been the person trying to convince the other person to go. It may take a little work, but nothing really good in life comes easy.

If you're single and you don't know what to do, re-read the chapter. Stop wasting time with random people and better yourself. Courting wasn't intended for you to have casual sex. Courting was supposed to be two people meeting to see if they have things in common, like religion, hobbies, family, and if they do, it leads to a loving marriage. I'll get into that a little deeper later. But use this

> *Courting wasn't intended for you to have casual sex.*

alone time you hate to better yourself and prepare yourself to be a great wife. Heal the demons you're pulling through life from your youth, family, and bad choices. Then when you meet Mr. "I Want To Spend The Rest Of My Life With You," you're ready. All of you need to talk to someone to heal those mental, spiritual, and emotional issues you've encountered throughout life. Work on your relationship and yourself so every day is the life you look forward to!

"May he give you the desire of your heart and make all your plans succeed" (Psalms 20:4 NIV).

CAN WE GET RID OF
THE HO PHASE?

*A*re you a lemon? I didn't say lemonade. I asked, are you a lemon? Ponder on that question for a minute. I'll come back to that. Can I ask you another question? Can we get rid of the ho phase, please? Pretty please? Pretty please with a cherry on top? Yeah, I know a lot of you will say, "A lot of women go through the ho phase; it's not a big deal!" Then you make it very clear to us men that you're not a ho!

"Don't call me a ho!"

"I ain't never been a ho!"

"Yo, momma may be a ho, but I'm not!" And you all wonder why men don't understand you.

How can you have a ho phase, and at the same time, say you're not a ho? Can an alcoholic stop drinking alcohol and not be an alcoholic? I think not! Ladies, I know you don't want to get rid of the ho phase. Who would? It's the perfect excuse for all of the men (and women) you've slept with in the past. It's a get-out-of-jail-free card for all of your past mistakes and lustful desires. It's the perfect excuse for all of the failed "situationships" that never progressed into relationships or marriage. It's the perfect comeback for any man who tells you that another man said, "Yeah, I used to hit shorty," or "My boy used to smash her," or "I got head from her." Or the most common response from men these days, "Hold up, I got a picture of her!"

If you cringed, it's because you know the picture he is about to show your man, your man's friend, or some guy you just met, is a picture of you that is best suited for Playboy, Pornhub, or OnlyFans. The ho phase is the perfect excuse for any man who asks you about a guy you used to sleep with who wasn't your boyfriend. It's the perfect excuse for the video Tyrone has of you in his phone. Lord knows we men *never* delete those pictures and videos. I may have videos saved from 2005 in my phone, email, or saved on a hard drive.

But the ho phase is a convenient excuse for that morning walk of shame many of you gallop down. What an adrenaline rush you must have as you are leaving a hotel or his place, going down the elevator, hoping none of his neighbors get on and see his dried-up semen on your dress. Your heels are in your hand while you act as if you're texting someone so you don't have to look up at the old lady who just got on the elevator to go to church. As the elevator slows down and the door opens, your inner voice is screaming, "NO!" The elevator stops again and more people get on. You're the only person on the elevator with last night's club clothes on, smelling like Tequila or Hennessey at 1 p.m. on a Sunday. You thank God for finally making it downstairs to your car or the Uber he ordered for you.

What a lady! I'm sorry. Is that your definition of a lady? I mean, I only ask because you said during this phase of your life you were a ho. Were you a ho? Can I ask you an honest question? Why do you get so mad when someone calls you a ho if at one point in your life you were proud to be a ho? Don't act like you weren't proud, babe. As soon as you got in that car, you immediately called or texted your girl and told her all about that good or bad d*ck you got last night. You usually call yourselves the "B" word when addressing one another, but that's another conversation to be had later. You all glorify all the ho phase activities you and the guy did last night. You give your girl the scoop from the sex to his car, his home, his furniture, if he has a friend for her, and maybe even what he did or didn't have in his refrigerator. It doesn't matter if

> *Why do you get so mad when someone calls you a ho if at one point in your life you were proud to be a ho?*

the story was good or bad about him, your p*ssy is always the best, right? (lol!)

I won't lie to you. It is the best p*ssy around until we cum. Unfortunately, once we cum, nut, or orgasm, whatever you want to call it, most of us are ready for the ho to go! Uber can't come fast enough for us. We will make any excuse known to man to get you away from us. We may have to go to Dubai to deliver Jay and Bey's Asian quintuplets. We will do or say anything to get you out of our house or us out of yours. We may start a five-alarm fire if it means we can get rid of you before the woman we love, who has been looking for us, calls and text us one more time. We love your ho phase, but it isn't worth losing the woman we love. By the way, we don't know Jay and Bey, nor are they having Asian babies. Nor have we delivered anything but penis to insecure, broken women, usually in their ho phase, after the club closes.

I'm not "slut-shaming." Wow! I would have never imagined a day where you couldn't shame a slut. Imagine a day when women are defending the sluts sleeping with their men and preventing the men they want to settle down from settling down and being loyal husbands and fathers. You have to stop conducting yourselves like Cardi B and expecting men to treat you like Beyoncé. Despite what her husband may or may not have done, Bey has always conducted herself like a queen. Have we left the days when women looked up to Phylicia Rashad and instead want to emulate women on Backpage? I support feminism, but I don't support feminists who equate feminism to strumpets. Slut-shaming is frowned upon if men are doing it, but if you catch a woman sleeping with your man, isn't it slut-shaming when you call the woman a ho, whore, or slut and attack the woman for doing what she *chose* to do with her body with *your* man?

Don't get me wrong, some of you end up with the guy you slept with after the club closed. Sometimes the guy likes the sex and wants to get to know you better. I hope you caught that. He didn't like you. He didn't know you that well. You didn't know him either. You may have been infatuated with the way he looked, talked, dressed or by what he drove, but you didn't like him. You didn't know him. He may have thought you were cool, pretty, fun, had a great a**, or rack, but he didn't like you.

"You" is the person you are internally. "You" isn't solely about your exterior. We all have our superlatives. I like to think of our superlatives as the things that initially attract us to a person. Anything that draws us to people that isn't their character, morals, mind, spirit, and heart are superlatives. The superlatives men are attracted to about women are usually physical. The superlatives women usually love about men are financial and physical. Take a moment and picture a man being the car of your dreams with all the upgrades you could wish for. It appears to be the car of your dreams, right? It has heated and cooled seats, a rearview camera, a side-view camera, massaging seats, panoramic roof, leather seats, drive-assist, and mink floors. The first thing you think is, this car is the one I want! Everyone will love and want my car, so you buy it. You're so happy leaving the car lot in your new car. You stop by all of your friends and family's houses to show it off. You picture the trips you'll take with your new car. You cruise through the mall, the place you grew up, and pull up at Quik Trip, hoping someone you know will see you in your new car. Everyone is happy and excited for you and your new car. Some people are even jealous on the low.

Soon thereafter, your car has problems. The panoramic roof gets stuck open on a rainy day. The heated seats don't heat up on the coldest day of the year. It's frustrating, and you're a little let down about your new car, but you get the little things you liked repaired, and you're happy again! Then after a little more time goes by, you notice your leather seats are cracking, and your rearview camera doesn't work, then the car breaks down. Slowly, but surely, everything you loved about the car's exterior doesn't seem so great. Why? You never looked at the engine, tires, transmission, and miles on the car. The most important parts of a car are under the hood. In the same way, the most important parts of a person are on the inside. You didn't look at what was inside. You focused on the outside, but baby, those upgrades and amenities, *the superlatives*, don't keep a car running. The car, a.k.a. "man you thought was so great," is a lemon.

You rarely take the time to look under the hood when you meet a man, especially in the ho phase. Then, one day when you need that special person in your life to be there for you emotionally, you get upset when he fails. You're let down by the fact that he isn't as perfect as you'd hoped he'd be. These are the lemons you constantly meet and accept into your lives. No matter how good he seems when you meet him, there's always something wrong with him in the end. Some of you reading this may be lemons yourselves.

Are you consumed with red bottoms, bags, clothes, perfume, jewelry, Poshmark, social media, YouTube, vlogs, Pinterest, Stiletto nails, skin, hair, and the shape of your body? Do you spend more time perfecting your exterior than you do your interior? If you lost it all today, would you feel comfortable that the man you like or love wouldn't leave you for someone who possesses those exterior things you no longer possess?

> *Do you spend more time perfecting your exterior than you do your interior?*

I'm not saying he would, but would you feel as confident as you do now? We all have bad days, but imagine if you had bad years.

Would your significant other stay with you and love you the same if you lost your car, job, credit, hair, clothes, and health? Ving Rhames once said some lines in this movie named *Baby Boy*. Maybe you've heard of it. He played this guy named Melvin, who told another guy named Jody, "You got to learn the difference between guns and butter. There two types of n***** in this world. There's n***** with guns and n***** with butter. Now, what are the guns? The guns, that's the real estate, the stocks, and bonds. Artwork, you know sh*t that appreciates with value. What's the butter?

Cars, clothes, jewelry, all that other bullsh*t that don't mean sh*t after you buy it."

Ving's character was speaking more about how we invest or waste our money. I think it also applies to what we invest or waste on ourselves as individuals. The time we spend focused on our accessories compared to our engine. The engine is the most important part of your car. I don't care what size rims you add, the engine is the most important part. The engine is a person's heart and spirit, who they truly are inside. The engine is what drives and maintains a relationship. It's who you are mentally, morally, and emotionally, a person's true character. These are the traits that determine if a person is a lemon or not. A person without these good qualities is a lemon. I know you spend a lot of time daily on your skin, hair, nails, and exterior. But your interior requires prayer, reading, studying, meditating, love, kindness, healing, growth, and God. My Muslim friends would call this "Deen over Dunyan." Deen over Dunyan means your faith and your spirit are more important than worldly things. Television and the Internet make you believe that worldly things are more important than they are.

Focusing solely on your exterior has made some of you lemons and that's why you keep meeting lemons. Some of you let persistent lemons convince you they are lemon pie when they are not. Remember, there's a distinct difference between a man who is *consistent* and a man who is *persistent*. Some of you let persistent lemons fool you into believing they were Beyoncé's "Lemonade." Not! So, I'll ask you again, "Do you have a good engine inside of you or are you a lemon?" Be honest. It's okay if you're a lemon. There's still time to add some sugar and water to your glass if you're willing to make some changes.

The change starts with you. It begins with recognizing your flaws and making a commitment to change your bad habits. Listen, it's important to understand that everyone who lets you down isn't a lemon, and just because you've let some people down, that doesn't mean you're a lemon. Truthfully, there may be many reasons he can't assist you when you need him to. He may have his own issues and problems, or maybe he's never had to help a person cope with the mental, emotional, physical, and spiritual issues you're dealing with.

> **The change starts with you.**

Sometimes people don't know what to do. That doesn't make a person a lemon. He may love and care for you deeply, but he may need you to communicate a little more than you want to about what you need or want from him.

I don't want you to read this book and break up with someone who genuinely loves you because he doesn't know how to be there for you the way you need him to be there for you in your time of need. If you're having this issue with someone, please find a good counselor to help you two find a resolution. A counselor will help you gain the positive qualities you need from each other in your relationship. Trust me, I'm sure he doesn't want to lose you, and I'm pretty sure he wants to be everything that you need. Unfortunately, people aren't born with all the great qualities their mate may need or want them to have. Some things must be asked for, taught, and learned over time. It may take a couple of times before they get it. Be patient and seek good counsel.

Sometimes, you learn at the most inopportune time that the person you like only wanted the physical parts of you. In that moment, you learn you are only another body to him. The exterior of your relationship looked good, but the interior, *the engine*, was not good; it was a lemon. Then there's the time you needed him to be there for you mentally or emotionally, and he was nowhere to be found. The sadder part is, he didn't want to be found. What an empty feeling! Don't get me wrong, some men purposely miss the moment you need them, and some don't know how to respond in the moment you need them. He loves you, but he doesn't know how or what to do. Sometimes, the person you've been sleeping with doesn't want to be there for you mentally or emotionally. He'll help you financially or physically, but that's as far as he'll go. I'm not speaking down on guys like me whose natural love language is giving gifts. We are getting better at quality time and acts of service.

Many men are gift-givers and bill helpers because we saw our mothers, the first women we loved, struggle and go without. I'm not talking about that guy. I'm talking about the guy who will pay a bill for a sexual thrill, but wants no other connection with you, especially when you need him to be there for you in your time of need.

Josephine, my amazing mother.

Unfortunately for you, that's usually the worst time to discover the engine is missing in your relationship. We all know that feeling—that hurt. You feel so empty inside. You feel used and you feel like a fool. The worst part is, you picked the car. You hopped in that big pretty car and mashed the gas. You failed to look the car over bumper-to-bumper, head-to-toe, and most of all, heart-to-mind. The heart, soul, and mind are the most important parts of a person. You have to take the time necessary to learn a person's strengths and weaknesses.

No one is perfect, but you can't find this out in the ho phase. The ho phase will only have you looking for an engine *after* you've purchased the car. You all know all about this, I'm sure! You find the person you like, but he doesn't possess all the things you want inside, so you start to "Build a Bear." You try to teach him all the things you'd like and want from a man. Ladies, you are not Dr. Frankenstein. You cannot build the man you want. It may work for a little while, but eventually, all you'll create is a monster. Either a monster you don't like, or a monster you can't get rid of.

> **No one is perfect, but you can't find this out in the ho phase.**

Some of you are driving cars that weren't for sale. Someone else already owns that car. He may be in a relationship or married. It's sad because a lot of you want to be in a faithful marriage, but you're knowingly sleeping with another woman's man. In the Bible, the question is posed: "You who say that people should not commit adultery, do you commit adultery?" (Romans 2:22 NIV).

Have you or someone you know slept with another woman's man? If so, what happened to women sticking together and girl power? Do you march and fight for equal rights, but not for monogamous homes? Do you only stand up against men who mistreat you and not the women breaking up homes and making it harder for you to find true love? You do know your ho phase affects other women trying to fall in love, get married, and have children, right? You do realize when you idly stand by, you're co-signing your friend, cousin, or sister sleeping with another woman's man, right? She's giving a man every reason not to settle down because of her endless supply of ho phase vagina. Her vagina doesn't require commitment from a man. Therefore, your co-sign on her lifestyle is aiding and assisting the gap in committed relationships. Without supply, there is no demand! I may speak on that later, but for now, I'll stick to the topic.

The ho phase has become a poor excuse for women to use when they're in a low place. It's a road some women take after they've been in a long marriage that ended or had children at a young age, and now they want to do all the things they couldn't do then. Sometimes it becomes a chosen path some women veer down after the death of someone close. Sex and alcohol are common coping mechanisms for depression. Some of you have been sexually abused, so you believe if you don't give him what he wants, he'll take it. So you allow him to have sex with you to avoid being forced to have sex and having your past trauma come back to mind. You've been made to feel like the villain and you're the victim. Please seek help, and if the person who victimized you hasn't been charged, please file charges no matter how long ago it may have been. I know it may be a hard memory to relive, and you may be embarrassed to face friends and family, but think about the little girl or boy you may save from this sick individual still walking the streets freely.

The ho phase is most infamously used after a breakup. Most people who have been heartbroken and scorned develop an "I don't care" mentality. But, usually after the sex, they feel horrible. I've felt terrible during ho phase sex. I've asked, *What are you doing? Why are you doing this? This is wrong. You should be home doing this with your old lady. Why are you doing this foul act that will hurt the person you genuinely love?* The ho phase serves no one. Well, I guess it serves its lustful purpose for the moment, but once it's over, it serves no one. And if the sex was bad, it *definitely* didn't serve you, right?

> **The ho phase serves no one.**

Wouldn't you much rather get to know the person with all the superlatives you admire to see if the superlatives go much deeper? I'm sure some of you are thinking to yourself, "Well, me and my one-night stand ended up together." That does happen, and that's great. I've experienced the same results. But, at some point in the relationship, usually at an insecure moment, you ask your partner, "Am I the only one-night stand you've had?" Whether they say yes or no, it's still a recurring thought for most people. Deep down inside, you know this person could sleep with someone they don't know or just met and never mention it. When they are out of town on a trip, you think about it. When they go to a nightclub, a bar, or even the grocery store, you know they can act on a sexual impulse with a person they just met.

The ho phase serves no one. It produces a promiscuous carnal lifestyle that may result in illegitimate children, rape, assault, insecurity, or worse. If you could go back in time and do it all over again, you both would probably choose not to have sex the first night you met and grow the relationship without the asterisk. What's the asterisk? The asterisk is the now hard question everyone asks: "How did you two meet?" In addition, doing so makes for a far easier conversation when your mother, father, or coworker asks you, "How did you two meet again?" Listen, I'm not judging you. I had my ho phase while I was single and in relationships. I've grown enough and reflected enough to know it was the wrong thing to do. I don't regret meeting one of my ex-girlfriends through a one-night stand. But, and I cannot emphasize this enough, the ho phase does not serve any of us.

Yeah, yeah, yeah, I know your ho phase wasn't as bad as your slutty friend or someone else you know. But hey, let me be clear. I dated a girl, and in the early stages of our relationship, she would always say, "Yeah, I had my ho phase! So, what! My past isn't as bad as so and so!" I told her never compare herself to someone else. I said, "Do you think you're better than her? That's like a steak comparing itself to bologna. Do you think you're better than the pig because the pig is lying in the mud and the cow is standing in the dirt? They're both dirty. The pig is just more comfortable in the dirt than the cow is. They're both serving the same purpose. Don't justify your standards by comparing them to what someone else may be doing." We all know a girl who says, "I'm not that bad. I know girls with way more bodies than me!" Don't ever compare yourself to trash. Be a leader in your life. Set a standard for yourself and be an example for those you love and those who look up to you. It doesn't matter if you were the high school, college, or neighborhood ho. It doesn't matter if you were stripping, looking for love in all the wrong places, or rebelling against your parents. Oh, and it doesn't make it better if you just want to do what men get to do all the time.

A while back, I talked to a friend who told me about how she slept with a guy I know. She told me how the guy (Guy #1) was telling some of his friends how he smashed her after the club one night. Little did he know one of the guys (Guy #2) who heard him telling the story was sleeping with her too. Unbeknownst to Guy #1, Guy #2 went back to her and told her what Guy #1 was telling his friends about her. (Side note: That's lame. You can't be in the ho phase loop and get in your feelings about the ho, bruh! (lol!) He must not have heard the phrase, "these hos for everybody.") Okay, back to the story. She told me how Guy #2 called her and told her what Guy #1 was telling his friends about her. So she went to the place where Guy #1 and his friends hung out. She said she walked in, and they all got quiet. She said she told Guy #1, "You didn't f**k me! I f***ed you, n****!!!" I thought that was so funny at the time. We seem to think that because we are the man in the situation, we are in control. But, often, the woman chose us long before we ever chose her.

Ladies, don't be men. Please! We have so much further to go than you do. Don't sink to our level, please. Sex is good. Don't get me wrong. But it's better with someone you have an emotional bond with. Someone you love and have dated.

> *Ladies, don't be men. Please!*

It took me a long time to realize that. Some of you can become emotionally tied with a guy in a couple of months or a year. I use the word "tied" because we all know when something is tied like your shoestrings, a rope, or a tie knot, it can come loose. Usually, it comes loose when stepped on, pulled, pushed, grabbed, or it wasn't tied as tight as we thought. Sometimes you unloosen the tie because you want a new or better tie. Sometimes you remove the tie simply because you don't like it anymore.

My point is, being emotionally tied to someone doesn't mean it'll last forever. Some of you become emotionally tied after a couple of weeks. You can become tied to someone mentally, sexually, emotionally, or spiritually. Some of you have even become financially tied to someone. Financial ties usually fall apart the fastest.

We all know the wife who left the husband because he couldn't afford her lifestyle anymore. We all know the man who left his wife after twenty years because he met someone who better matched his career path. If you're waiting on a financial tie, you'll probably be single for a while or end up alone. Money and love usually are billed by the hour. My point is, ties and attachments can come loose or be broken.

You want to bond with someone mentally, emotionally, and spiritually *over time*. I hope you noticed I left out sexually. It was purposely left out. Sex is supposed to be the final bonding element of a relationship, but nowadays, it's become an additive that usually weakens the bond between two people instead of strengthening the bond between two people. You want two strong, clean, and pure metals. The two metals represent you and your significant other. At the right point in your relationship, melt down the two metals you represent and blend them into one unique, pure metal. One solid love! That's a real bond. Once the metal is settled and cooled, mold it into two rings—a wedding band for him and a wedding ring for you. The bond between you two should be unbreakable! It should be unbreakable because you two took the time to get to know one another mentally, emotionally, spiritually, and financially *before* you became sexually intimate. You saved something special for the ultimate vow of love. "A wife of noble character who can find? She is worth far more than rubies" (Proverbs 31:10 NIV).

I've come to a point in my life that I don't want sex until I know this woman is the one I will spend the rest of my life with. The one I will remain faithful to. The one who I've taken the time to know inside and out before we give ourselves to one another. I've had emotionally-bonded sex. I've had physical sex. I've had ho phase sex. I've had f**k buddy sex. And you know I've had one-night-stand sex. But I've never had this-is-my wife sex. I want sex with something under the hood. I want to own the title and add all the up-grades we want together. I want mental, physical, spiritual, and emotional love and sex. I want a connection, but we've all connected with many people. We've even connected with a few people during our ho phase. That's how they ended up getting our goodies. Now, I want more than just a con-nection. Say it with me: We want the engine! I don't know if you want a new engine, old engine, or to rebuild an engine, but you do. So again, I'll ask you, "Can we get rid of the ho phase?"

WHERE'S THE COW?

*P*ardon me. Do you know where I can find "the cow?" I've been looking for it for some time now, but I'm wondering if it even exists. Yes, I'm talking to you. Yes, you, the one reading this book. Where's the cow? I'm sorry, do you only provide a carton of milk at a time? Do you like "Vitamin D" only? Do you prefer a straw in your milk or do you prefer your milk drank like a cat lapping? Which flavor cow are you? Chocolate milk? White milk? Almond milk? Soymilk? Chai milk? Skim milk? Goat milk? Oat milk? Rice milk? Coconut milk? Raw milk? Hmm. I bet a lot of you are raw milk. Are any of you whole milk?

I've been looking for whole milk, too. No, actually, I'm looking for the whole cow. Have you seen a whole cow? I don't want the carton. I heard I could get a whole gallon. I don't want that. I want the whole cow. I've had a few flavors of those cartons of milk in the past. They're okay. But everybody's tried them at least once. I want the whole cow. Has anyone seen the whole cow? I've heard people talk about the whole cow. I've been promised the whole cow, but I've never had one. I know people who had a whole cow. Some of their cows got away, though. Some of the whole cows who stayed with their men provided their men carton milk too. So again, I'll ask, "Have any of you seen a whole cow?" Don't you all speak up at once. My bad. I forgot.

Most women are giving away the milk, but you're saving the cow for your husband. Woohoo! Or should I say, "Yoo-hoo!"? (lol!) Well, isn't he lucky! That was sarcasm by the way. You've been giving away his fresh milk glass by glass, and for some, gallon by gallon for years to any suitable patron. But now, your husband, your true love, your soul mate, Mr. "I Want To Spend The Rest Of My Life With You" gets to have that beat up, tired, exhausted, used, abused, tested, vaccinated, unvaccinated, loose, drippy, dry, vibrated, penetrated, baggy, not as tight as it used to be, pulled on, stitched up, pushed in, grabbed, slapped, licked, fingered, smelly, bit, broken, scarred, torn, burned, bruised, passed around lazy cow you've been saving until he makes you his wife! Here she is! I found the cow, everybody!

> **Most women are giving away the milk, but you're saving the cow for your husband.**

So this is what you've been saving all your life for your husband. Forgive me; I'm wrong. The p*ssy was expendable. Cooking, cleaning, and homemaking duties are what you're saving for your husband.

What's the famous line you like to say, ladies? "I have to save something for my husband." So, let me get this right. Men can have your sex, oral sex, anal sex, and even ménages with you, but cooking and cleaning are off the table! (lol!) A man can explore every part of your body physically and sexually, but he has to put a ring on your finger before you do things a wife would do. I'll be honest. I'd much rather you get up every morning and cook breakfast for the man you're dating than give him my soon-to-be wife's mouth and vagina every morning for breakfast. I'd much rather you keep the house clean for him than let him hit it from the back and smack my precious soon-to-be wife's a** until it's red, purple, and bruised. I'd much rather you clean the bathroom and sweep the floor occasionally than send him nude pictures and videos of my soon-to-be wife he will save and have forever on his iCloud and WhatsApp. Oh, my bad, you sent it on SnapChat and it disappeared, right?

I know you all will say that was in the past, but beloved, those nude pictures and videos are in the present. Please don't miss my point looking for an excuse or reason for your actions. Is the cow more important than the milk or is the milk more important than the cow? If you haven't caught on to my metaphors and similes yet, the milk is your vagina. The cow is everything else you could offer to the relationship, except for sex. Listen, I don't want my wife to give away the cow or the milk. But I know that's not our reality, unfortunately. I'm sure a man would prefer his wife wash and fold clothes for her ex instead of trying anal for the first time. I know you say you love me more, but besides your words, he and I got the same sexual actions. Also, you were loyal and in love with him as well at the time. He just chose not to propose to you. I can't blame him. He got the milk without the responsibilities of the cow.

Ladies, you say you're saving something for your husband, right? What are you saving? Yes, he gets to give you a ring. He gets to watch you walk down the aisle to him. He gets to tell you I do and kiss you in front of all of your aunts and co-workers waiting anxiously for you to finally get married. I know you will make love to him for the first time as his wife. That's great.

What are you saving?

But that's all a ritual. You will not make love to him every time you have sex like it's the night of your honeymoon. I know you all love to say I will be my husband's hooker, friend, wife, and his cook. His everything. LIE! That'll last about a week. A wise man once told me, "The person you were before the wedding, you'll be less than after the wedding." Dare I remind you, you've already been most of those things you swear you will be for your husband for someone who didn't have to buy you a wedding ring, nor did he have to carry you over the threshold. So, I'll ask you again, "What are you saving for your husband?"

May I remind you the most important part of the marriage ritual is the gift of your chastity. It isn't your cooking and cleaning. It isn't your submission. Somewhere along the lines, you ladies made a bad trade. Now we are where we are, and we can't go backward. But, d*mn. Chastity was the motivation for men to marry a woman. In the past, I'm sure men weren't lining up to marry a woman

> *May I remind you the most important part of the marriage ritual is the gift of your chastity.*

with five, ten, twenty and fifty plus sexual partners. Those numbers don't include the guys who only gave you oral sex or you only gave them oral sex.

Our great grandfathers, grandfathers and fathers went to brothels to find women like that. That's where men went to find women who gave away their milk to men for money or notoriety. Nowadays, that's the normal. You all actually defend it. Some of you defend yourselves by comparing yourself to a man.

Whoa! I just imagined a cat taking a number two on your living room floor and playing in it and telling you, "It's okay. The dog does it all the time." I'm not a cat lover, but I know a cat would never sink as low as a dog's way of life. But I guess nowadays a Ruth's Chris dinner, a Louie Vuitton bag, or a trip buys a man a glass of your milk. Is this the new prostitution? A man can buy you dinner or spend money on you and he gets to have your cookie? A couple good dates and conversations and someone's daughter's legs are going up like it's 12 o'clock. Sometimes it only takes a couple shots of top-shelf liquor and you're on your way home to claim another body.

The stock price of cow milk isn't worth much nowadays and the stock in the cow providing the milk is even lower. Which reminds me, the Bible says, "Help, Lord, for no one is faithful anymore; those who are loyal have vanished from the human race" (Psalms 12:1 NIV). Maybe your milk's still valuable to some sucker or seat filler. I'm not saying someone won't marry you. But wouldn't you feel much better knowing your milk is organic? If I were a bull, I'd feel more confident knowing all the other bulls on the ranch haven't tasted my lady's sweet milk. Nor do they have pictures to pass around whenever my lady's name comes up. However, these are the times we're living in. And you all have the nerve to call yourselves ladies. And if you are a lady, how dare you let these women call themselves a lady. You should be ashamed and have more pride in what you represent.

Do you know the definition of a lady? There are many definitions, but none call a lady a casual sex partner or prostitute. If you don't know the definitions, here are the definitions for a lady: "a woman of superior social position, especially one of noble birth"

> **Do you know the definition of a lady?**

or "a man's wife." Are you one of these definitions? Hold up, before you answer that question, please let me define "noble." Noble is defined as "belonging to a hereditary class with high social or political status, aristocratic" or "having or showing fine personal qualities or high moral principles and ideals." So, again, I'll ask you, "Are you a lady? Did you notice none of the definitions listed above say your actions are okay because a man can do it? Nor do they say your actions are okay because you're not as bad as some women you may know. You see words like high morals, superior social position, and noble. Do you think you're exhibiting a high social position if a man can potentially show a video of you performing fellatio on him to your husband? Does that reflect high morals or noble characteristics? Some of you have pictures and videos in several men's phones and emails. What happened, ladies? When did you lose hope? When did instant gratification become more important than waiting for your wedding date? When did an orgasm become more important than the sanctity of marriage?

I'm pretty sure most of you wish you could go back and unf**k the person who took your virginity. You may want to erase your second and third sexual experiences, too. I understand peer pressure and the pressure to fit in may have influenced some of those decisions. I understand curiosity and the urge we all felt as we got older made you make poor choices. Then there's so much sex on TV, websites like Pornhub, and social media that make us horny all the time. I understand, but beloved, you're jumping into every relationship and giving away one of the most important parts of the vow of marriage. I'm trying to understand how you expect a man to marry you and be full of pride while you've given away one of the main reasons he's marrying you to multiple trials and errors.

In the past, men married a woman for her help and loyalty, the cow. Besides that, those men were able to be the first man to remove her chastity belt and enter her womb, the milk. I know you can't go back in time, but it's not too late to start over. Stop! Then encourage your girlfriend to stop. Encourage your nieces and daughters to wait and tell them your war stories and the reasons they should wait. Tell them how much you regret your first time. Tell them how many men you regret sleeping with. Tell them how much you wish you waited until you got married to have sex. Tell them to hone their skills at being a better woman and potential wife.

> *I know you can't go back in time, but it's not too late to start over.*

It's okay to display your skills at being a potential wife for a man. It's far better and less risky than displaying your skills at being a bedroom freak for every man you thought you liked or loved.

Do me a favor. Grab a pen and a piece of paper. Write down a list of ten women close to you or who are close to women you know. Write beside each of their names whether they are single, engaged, or married. Then write their ages beside their names. Then write beside their names if they are faithful or unfaithful. I think you'll be surprised at how few of them are truly happily married and faithful. The rest of them are in the same casual dating sex pool you're swimming in. Your odds of finding a happy marriage in that swamp you call a dating pool are low. Yes, I said a swamp. That's what casual sex and serial dating should be called—the swamp. You may want to stop swimming in that dirty pool before you drown. I know you all are probably thinking men will hate him. He's telling us to stop having sex with our boyfriend, boo, or hook up. Why is he telling us to stop having casual sex and he's a man?

Beloved, I know no matter what, there will always be women for men to take advantage of. I also know, no matter how many jewels I give women, some of you will still give your milk to men just because of the man he is or the man you think he is. I'm a real man, but I'm also a real n****. Real n***** want you all to do better. We don't want a woman who has been with a n**** we know or don't like. We don't want a woman who has been with some cornball who looks up to us and now he can say I had your woman. Some men only want to sleep with you because you used to date or sleep with a man he secretly envies or looks up to. Sounds crazy, but it happens. Take, for example, the numerous celebrities who can have almost any woman they want, but they date the same girl some other celebrity used to date. Sadly, some women become a trophy that some men only want to sleep with to feel like they've made it to a certain social status.

Real men don't want a woman like that. Real men want their lady to be just that, a lady. Yes, we have to do better. I know. Trust me, we know. I also know everything a man does is for the attention of a woman. So, if you all require more time, attention, and respect from us instead of the routine schedule of casual sex, that's what we will give you. If the new trend is you have to marry a woman to have sex or receive oral sex, guess what we will start doing? Yep, we will start getting married. But, if the trend is to put on a necklace, pop some bottles, wear designer clothes, have money, and you get loads of p***y, guess what? That's what we will do. Sound familiar?

> **Real men want their lady to be just that, a lady.**

There's a phrase I've heard a few times. Maybe you've heard it before: "If you want something different, you have to do something different." Most of you are doing the exact same thing, man after man, and you're expecting different results. You're not solely responsible for fixing the gap in our generation's relationships, but men will follow a woman's lead, even if it leads us to bite the forbidden fruit. Just ask Eve. Lord knows you all are dealing with enough and now I'm asking you to take the lead in your quest for true love and for true happiness. A lot of you aren't happy. Years and years of failed relationships made you vulnerable and led you to being played, used, and abused. Now you're bitter, resentful, insecure, and distrustful of men and relationships. Guess what you feel like now? Spoiled milk!

You're not spoiled milk, sweetheart. Your expiration date hasn't arrived yet. I know you're fed up and now you have the mentality that you will do men the exact same way they do women! Although I understand your position, it'll never work. That mentality only helps the man get more milk without the responsibility of owning the cow. Not that a man will own you. Nor are you literally a cow. Please, don't beat me up. (lol!) I'm just trying to help. Let's let go of the spoiled milk mentality. The spoiled milk mentality is the mentality a lot of women

> **You're not spoiled milk, sweetheart.**

have adopted after a failed marriage, relationship, or being played by someone they liked. You stop caring. You start feeling low. You just want to have fun and do the things you couldn't do or didn't do in your past relationships. You have random sex and serial date. You're hoping in the midst of all the dating and sex you somehow meet Mr. "I Want To Spend The Rest Of My Life With You." A few of you have, luckily! But most of you meet a lot of guys, sleeping with a portion, and end up home alone. Yeah, you get to go on some amazing trips, eat fantastic meals, and fatten up your closet with some of Italy's and Paris's best designers.

Along the way, you meet doctors, lawyers, bankers, truckers, drug dealers, entrepreneurs, and entertainers. It seems exciting until you think about the doctor with the nice house, but he had a little d*ck. The drug dealer with the killer personality, but he had no 401k. The lawyer with the huge penis, but his wife sent you a message on Facebook Messenger while you and her husband were away in Miami. What about the successful and handsome VP who made upper six figures and had you move in and play house and everyone was so happy for you, but they didn't know he was beating you like you were a man every chance he got. We can't forget about the NFL player who your mom was so excited to tell everyone you were dating, until you discovered you were just one of his many girlfriends waiting to be with him after the game on Sunday. Sorry, Mom!

Now you feel like you're stuck. You're tired of asking God for a good man. You're tired of watching other women have babies. You're tired of seeing other women post their wedding pictures on your timeline. You give up. You do what makes you happy. But none of the things that come with your promiscuous lifestyle truly make you happy. You have far more failures than successes. You feel like spoiled milk. You're not.

You are the whole cow. You just have to take more pride in your milk. You have to choose to be a glass of milk or a wife. You can still date and enjoy meeting new people. You don't have to tell every man I'm not having sex until I meet my husband. Although this may be true, it could make a man feel like you're pressuring him into marriage and you may run off Mr. "I Want To Spend The Rest Of My Life With You." Men like to feel like the option of sex is still on the table, even if it isn't at the moment. If you meet someone and the relationship grows, he will eventually catch the hint you are different, have a vision, and want more out of life than just sex and a good time. If he wants to get to know you more, he will continue to court you and continue to grow the relationship. Some men will walk away, and it may be someone you liked. It may hurt. You'll have to look at the bigger picture and accept the outcome. But trust me, it will not hurt as much as him curving you after you have given him your glass of milk.

> **If you meet the right man, he will have conversations with you about what you want in life.**

If you meet the right man, he will have conversations with you about what you want in life, what he wants in life, what you both want in a relationship, and maybe even marriage. So, go out and enjoy dating and getting to know men, all the while knowing you won't be having sex with him at the end of the night just because he treated you to dinner and made you giggle a few times. That's the whole cow mentality. The whole cow mentality is focusing on the long-term goal of marriage and not the short-term goal of a nut. Let's not worry about what men should or shouldn't be doing at this moment.

We all know men have to be held accountable. Don't let another person's poor actions or lack thereof sway your actions to better your mind, heart, and spirit. I want you to worry about your own growth and accountability for now. This change and growth is for you! Maybe one day it will be for him, but for now, you're the star of the show. You're beginning the journey of saving something for the most important and special person in your future life—your husband. From this point on, no one else gets to sample the milk

> **You will no longer settle for less from yourself or a man.**

from this cow. No one else gets to decide when, where, and how you serve your milk. You will no longer settle for less from yourself or a man. Today, you'll start a new mission in life. This mission will require you to be a noble woman, a woman of superior social position, and a woman whose goal is to become a man's wife. A lady. You can change. "Therefore, if anyone is in Christ, the new creation has come: The old has gone, the new is here!" (2 Corinthians 5:17 NIV).

Some of you cannot give sex up completely. Some of you will minimize sex and substitute sex with toys. I get it. As a recovering sex addict who eventually got to where he made a vow of celibacy and to intentionally date only one woman, I understand how foreign it may sound to say, stop having sex. Trust me! I couldn't fathom not having sex or only dating one woman, but it's one of the best choices I've made in my life! Imagine being a person who wanted to have sex three to four times every day. I mean, every day. But along the journey from the streets to the music industry and the lifestyle of money, clothes, and hos, I finally reflected and saw how my lifestyle was affecting my relationship. I realized my actions were unfair to my partner. My poor decisions were inflicting pain, insecurity, and low self-esteem on someone I said I loved. I wasn't being the best example of a man for my mate, daughter, nieces, or sisters. I wasn't being the best version of myself for me, and most of all, God.

Okay, cow, meet bull. Do you know the life of a bull? I know that bulls fight, make a great-tasting steak, and are the stud for the cows on the farm. Yes, bulls lay the pipe to any cow they want. Sound familiar? I think so. Most men are raised as a bull is raised. We are raised to be strong and never back down from a fight. A lot of us are alpha males and some of us have a temper and see red when we get mad. But most of all, we are taught to sleep with as many women as we can, while we can, and if we can. So, most of our lives, we do just that. Women become objects and trophies for us to gain during our lives. The trophies may be how successful, pretty, thick, freaky, or popular the woman is. We will do and say whatever it takes to attain that trophy. Over time, we become masters of deception. This causes many of us to become misogynistic.

The more successful we become at sleeping with different women, the more narcissistic we become, usually. Our ego and pride fog the very light we need to see how wrong our decisions and lifestyles are with women and ourselves. Yes, ourselves. One of the greatest lessons I've learned through my counseling with Dr. Hannah is that I lacked respect for women who slept with multiple men, but I didn't recognize that I lacked the same respect for myself by allowing multiple women to sleep with me. I was sleeping with multiple women, all the while looking down on women for giving their bodies away to multiple men. I didn't realize I was doing the same thing. I actually had less respect for myself because I was allowing every woman who offered and appealed to me to have my "Vitamin D!" That's not cool.

> *I'm writing this because a drastic change is needed in how men and women view commitment.*

It's not cool for me, and sweetheart, it's not okay for you either. I'm writing this because a drastic change is needed in how men and women view commitment. Women are true leaders and possess a power over men that can positively change the course of future relationships. Men chase and women play hard to get. Well, at least you used to. I don't want you to run forever, but I do want your next lover to be your last lover and last forever. If things keep going the way they're going, we will all be a bunch of old, divorced, brokenhearted hos, and players.

However, I hope you all make the choice to pursue wholeness because until now, I'm sure you've left a lot of relationships and bedrooms feeling empty, incomplete, and lonely. So, sweetheart, please do something different so you don't end up an old lonely cow.

Oh, and fellas, if you're reading this. Don't ever call your lady a cow. 😌

ARE YOU A RUNAWAY?

*Y*our true love shows up on your wedding day and says, "Run away with me." What do you do? Maybe I went too deep, too soon. I wanted to catch you off guard. However, that is a real question. I want you to have an honest thought. I know you thought about it. You don't have to tell me the answer, but your heart knows the truth. I mean, if you're marrying your true love as you should be, you're running away together after the wedding anyway, right? But, if you have to think about what you would do if your true love showed up on your wedding day and asked you to run away with him, you

> **Your true love shows up on your wedding day and says, "Run away with me."**

must have said yes to the seat filler, instead of Mr. "I Want To Spend The Rest Of My Life With You."

Yeah, you can love the seat filler. You can be in love and marry the seat filler. You can have kids and make memories with the seat filler. Many people marry the seat filler, but the seat filler is the reason you're thinking about my question. Some of you reading this wish your true love did show up on your wedding day. My question made me think about the movie *Ocean's Eleven*. Do you remember when Danny Ocean came back to get his true love, Tess, at the beginning of the movie? She was very reluctant and rejected him. She was distraught, bitter, and resentful with his past choices in their relationship. Nowadays, we would say, "She was in her feelings!" Her new life seemed perfect and her new love was the wealthy and debonair Terry Benedict. She was living the dream. She was *happy*. But, do you remember the ending? If not, go back and watch the movie. Be careful what your feelings leave behind in life because you may have left your heart behind.

Forgive me, sometimes my mind is all over the place, but it always finds its way back. (lol!) Okay, so let me try this again. You're out one night and you bump into your ex. You know the ex you've thought about occasionally when your man isn't around or you two are arguing and you say it's over! Some of you even picture him when you're having sex with the seat filler you fell in love with and married. The ex everyone knew you loved more than God's given air, but it didn't work out. The ex you were infatuated with for years,

Love Is The Agenda

and no matter how good life is, you still think about him. Sometimes it's innocent and sometimes it's not. You two are probably not together because of something he did that you couldn't forgive him for or you couldn't get over. Yes, him.

What happened when you saw him? Did you get stuck like a deer in headlights and you didn't know what to say or do? Did you imagine how your kids would've looked? Did you picture your wedding full of his friends and your friends taking the best wedding party pictures before the reception? Oh, and the house! I know you imagined the house. You two would've had to buy an enormous five-bedroom house with a big backyard for both of your family members to visit. Okay, so who would you call first to tell you bumped into your ex? Would you call your mom, your girlfriend, or would you keep it a secret? Maybe you wouldn't tell your mom because she would be against it.

> **What happened when you saw him?**

You may tell your girlfriend because she couldn't judge you since her love life is a complete mess. She would support whatever decision you made regardless of how smart or stupid it is. What could she possibly say anyway? She's a loyal side chick to a married man, all the while being a disloyal girlfriend in a dysfunctional "try sexual" relationship. You know what a "try sexual" relationship is, right? They'll "try" anything except a normal functioning relationship. I'm sure you know the type. The friend you say you love, but you stand by idly as she makes one bad decision after another. You think you're a good friend because you don't judge her and support her no matter how good or bad her choices may be. Hmm... but are you truly being a good friend? I don't think so. A true friend or best friend should hold the ones she loves and cares for accountable. You can't control her choices in life, but you don't have to agree with her choices either. You should be providing her with good counsel. And if you can't, you should be suggesting that she find good counsel. It's obvious there's a deeper demon and issue she's fighting that is the root of her dysfunctional behavior.

You know her choices aren't healthy, so as her friend, you should make that clear and hold her accountable by any means necessary. A true friend shouldn't be there just to like or love all of your poor choices. A true friend should be there to applaud you on the peaks and pull you out of the valleys. Some of you have friends who are silent or applauding you while you are in the valley. No one needs a friend like that. You need to re-evaluate your arena if that's the case. You don't have to cut them off, but you do need to let them know we have to be better and more accountable as friends.

Okay, let me get back to my point. Maybe you would call your mom. She's tired of you being alone anyway. She may support you finding a new love or trying to rekindle things with your past love. Maybe she's been ready for you to leave your current man. Things just aren't moving fast enough for her. Or maybe she thinks you could do better. I don't know. She may be sick of hearing you say you're leaving him, so now she's like, just do it already! You've been griping to her for years about how unhappy you are. You've been feeding your arena only the negative things about your mate for so long that they're totally against him now. They've been waiting on you to kick him to the curb and move on. They're loyal to you, so they solely rely on your side of the story. The things you feel are more than likely subjective, but they don't care. The things you've told them about your mate are probably based solely on your feelings, emotions, and your own beliefs. The information you provide people about your fragile relationship isn't necessarily the facts. You probably explain your side of the story with a lot of "I think" and "I feel." You probably embellish a little, but I won't be the one to call you a liar. You are entitled to your feelings, right? No one can tell you what you're feeling isn't true. Maybe some of it is, but a lot of it *is* subjective. It's feelings.

> **The things you've told them about your mate are probably based solely on your feelings, emotions, and your own beliefs.**

I once heard someone say, "Feelings aren't real." Then they told another person (Person 2), "Point to your arm," and Person 2 pointed to their arm. Then they told Person 2, "Point to your head," and Person 2 pointed to their head. Then they told Person 2, "Point to your feelings," and Person 2 paused, and said, "What?" They said, "Point to your feelings! Show me your feelings!" Person 2 smiled and said, "I can't. I can't point to my feelings." I was astonished at the entire exchange. It was a deep conversation. At that moment, I realized feelings don't exist. Well, feelings do exist because we have them, but they don't physically exist.

We have the power to be happy, mad, sad, or angry. Maybe that's why Peter said, "Cast all your anxiety on Him because He cares for you" (1 Peter 5:7 NIV). God knows we make irrational decisions based on our feelings, and that's why He told Peter to tell us to cast our feelings on Him, so we don't make a permanent decision based on temporary emotions. Cain killed Abel based on temporary feelings. David committed adultery with Bathsheba based on temporary feelings. Two bad decisions based on how people felt, temporarily, in that moment.

We can change our thoughts. That's easier for some of us to do than others. We can control our feelings. We all have heard these famous lines from children and friends and have probably said it ourselves in a relationship: "He hurt my feelings!" "She hurt my feelings!" Lord knows, being a very direct and blunt individual, I've been told I hurt someone's feelings a million times. If I've ever hurt your feelings, I apologize. God and I have been working overtime on my unpredictable mouth, I promise. But aside from that, do you want to know the definition of "hurt"? The definition of hurt is to "cause physical pain or injury to." Can you physically hurt something that doesn't physically exist? Do you know what "feeling" means? The definition of feeling is "an emotional state or reaction" or "a belief, especially a vague or irrational one." I'm sure we've all had an emotional reaction to something we thought or something we believed someone did. I'm also sure we've all had irrational feelings based on something we believed to be true.

Feelings are subjective. Yes, some things make us sad. For example, losing a loved one can make you sad, but someone else may be happy the deceased is no longer in pain. Getting a promotion at your job can make you happy, but if you expected a better promotion, the same promotion could make you feel sad or angry. Feelings are subjective, an opinion. Facts are objective. They are indisputable. They exist. Am I writing this book? Yes.

Do me a favor and picture this. Picture someone blowing the horn at you in your car and you reacting and flipping your middle finger at the person who blew the horn at you. Did the person deserve the middle finger? No. I'll explain why the feeling that provoked your reaction was wrong. Imagine you're pulling out of a parking spot and someone is waiting on your spot, but it's taking you a little longer than normal to back out of the spot. When you finally back up and you're about to pull forward, the driver of the car waiting on your parking spot taps the horn at you. Then you get mad because the driver blew their horn at you and you think they did it because you took too long to back out of the parking spot, so you give the person the middle finger and yell something obscene. As you drive off, you come to a stop sign and someone walking by signals you to roll down your window.

Once you roll down your window, the person walking by says, "Hey, you left your Starbucks cup on the top of your car." You say, "Oh! Thank you!" Immediately, you realize you just flipped off someone because you felt like the person blew their horn at you because you were taking too long to back out of a parking space. However, the person was only trying to tell you that you left your Starbucks coffee on the top of your car.

Do you see how your subjective feelings can be wrong? Do you see how quickly you can react before you assess things? Do you see how you can react incorrectly to something *you* thought was right? Do you see how your interpretation of something can be wrong? Do you see how your feelings escalated due to irrational thoughts and a vague belief that someone was doing something they were not doing?

> **When we don't understand something or don't have all the facts, we assume and those assumptions lead to feelings we believe are correct.**

When we don't understand something or don't have all the facts, we assume and those assumptions lead to feelings we believe are correct. Now I want you to think about all the times you felt your partner should have known to do something or all the times you felt your partner did something on purpose. How often did you take something your partner said wrong? How often did you feel like your partner should have known what to do without you telling him? How often did you assume and believe something based on feelings and not facts? How often did you think negative thoughts about your partner based on subjective feelings? Those subjective feelings have now led you to cheating. Do you really think the relationship with the person you're cheating with is going to last? Can I give you a word of advice? Don't cheat. It only taints your crown, as well as your king's crown. If you're dating, in a relationship, married, or telling someone you love him, don't cheat. Don't entertain an ex or someone new who seems like a breath of fresh air.

We've all done it. We've all given someone our number, email or business card when we knew we were in some form of relationship with someone else. I understand relationships get bad. I understand relationships get boring. I also understand sometimes relationships aren't moving the way we want or expect them to. Can I tell you something? Most of the time, the person you're about to cheat on, or you are cheating on, wants things to be better in your relationship too! He just doesn't know how to fix it, but he wants to. And guess what? You obviously don't know how to fix it either or you wouldn't be cheating or about to cheat.

There are relationships where the other person doesn't want to fix the relationship and that's a relationship you need to end maturely. Not after you've met someone else, talked on the phone, been on a date, and maybe had sex with him. Not after you've made sure he is someone you really want and now it's safe to break up with the person you said you loved. Is that love? Is that caring? Is that how you want to be treated? I'm sure it's the exact opposite of what you would want the person you love to do to you. A lot of you have had your hearts broken by someone doing the same thing to you. Now you're doing or about to do the same thing to someone else. As my daughter would say, "Shameful!"

It's okay to break up. It's okay to have changed feelings for someone. It's okay to outgrow someone. It's okay to fall out of love. It's okay to be done. Just show some character and common decency when you do it. Even if you feel the person you're dealing with will not do the same for you, be the bigger spirit. Good character isn't based on what someone else will or will not do. Good character is based on *your* integrity and integrity is doing the right thing when no one is around or looking. "Whoever walks in integrity, walks securely, but whoever takes crooked paths will be found out" (Proverbs 10:9 NIV).

> *For generations, we have watched our elders run away from relationships with excuses and maybe start rebound relationships.*

For generations, we have watched our elders run away from relationships with excuses and start rebound relationships. This has left the world with countless amounts of broken homes, parentless children, and very few examples of healthy relationships. I'm not telling you to stay. I'm telling you to exit the right way. Most of us have heard the saying, "The easiest way to get over something is to get under something." My friend, Marqui, was the first person I heard say that and he said it to me. God bless his soul, and may he rest in peace. He saw me hurting, and he mentioned it one day when we were riding around, probably hustling. He didn't tell me to do it, but he did mention it. I didn't do it, but I have watched many people do that very thing—start a rebound relationship. Most didn't end up with the person they got under.

I'll tell you the truth. Most went back to the person they were trying to get over. Or, the person they ended up under or with, always knew they were still in love with their ex when they hooked up and got under them. So, no matter what, there was always a trust issue in their relationship. Despite what was done or said, deep down inside, they knew they were initially a rebound. Yes, the love may have grown and good memories may have been made, but they always knew the beginning of their love story began as a rebound. They know the first time you two made love, you thought about your ex before, during, or after.

We all know about rebound relationships or have been in a rebound relationship. We also know many fail, and that some last for a moment and fewer last for years. Most rebound relationships start because someone left a relationship that was filled with drama, trauma, and uncertainty. We must not forget, most rebounds you meet are full of sh*t! Most rebounds are professional actors who will listen, learn, and adapt to be everything you said your ex wasn't in your past relationship. How many people have discovered days, months, or years later that the person they thought they knew was a complete fraud? Have you ever watched the movie, *The Talented Mr. Ripley*? Some of you are falling in love with him right now. I've heard so many war stories of women meeting men who promised them the world and couldn't afford a trip to Mickey D's. I know some men who will groom a vulnerable woman looking for love in all the wrong places for months and even years just to get what they want. Sometimes they want sex and sometimes they want money.

The rebound can also have money but still be a fraud. I know of a guy who was the rebound for a girl trying to get over her ex. After a few months of dates, trips, and extravagant gifts, he proposed. She thought he was such a gentleman and bragged about him to all of her friends. He never once propositioned her for sex while they were dating. Unfortunately, on the night of their wedding, she found out he couldn't consummate the marriage. He was impotent. Guess who she ended up with after the marriage was annulled? Her ex! Thank God she didn't giveaway her goodies to a fraud! Even though she was ready and willing to. (smh!)

I could tell you so many horror stories, but we need to dissolve rebound relationships, long story short. More times than not, they serve the man, not the woman. Rebound relationships usually fascinate someone who is insecure and looking for validation. If you're someone who has met your last two to three mates while still with or dealing with your ex, your issue is deeper than just cheating. "For an adulterous woman is a deep pit" (Proverbs 23:27 NIV). You need to learn how to end relationships in a grown and mature manner. A break-up doesn't always have to end messy and drama-filled.

You also need to learn how to effectively work on resolving your relationship issues. If you have an issue with your mate, immediately resolve it. Don't go out and bump into someone who seems like the light to your darkness. If you're ready to end a relationship, end it. Don't keep going back and forth, breaking up and making up. That usually confuses the other person when you're really ready to move on. You've left and came back 100 times and now you want him to believe that this time, you're seriously done because you've met and secured someone new. A person he has no idea you've already been building and dealing with while sleeping with him. You don't have to come back for round 101 this time because you made sure you had a sound rebound. Classy!

> *You also need to learn how to effectively work on resolving your relationship issues.*

Please pardon my sarcasm, but you did just cheat. You didn't cheat? You two weren't together? You didn't have sex with him before you met the rebound? You didn't have sex with him after you met the rebound? You weren't talking and texting with him at the same time you were talking to the rebound? The moment you passed your card or gave your phone number to the rebound, you cheated. I know you think you didn't cheat or do anything wrong because you've been telling him you're not happy, you want more, asking what are we doing, etc. But, baby, you're cheating. Your new boo was your side piece before he was officially your new boo. How? The entire time you were talking to the rebound, you were telling your current boo you're not happy, you want more, asking what are we doing, etc. You were also telling him you love him and hoped things would change and confiding in him, all while secretly talking to someone else—the rebound. Now the rebound is the new boo. I know you think it wasn't the old boo's business, but it was.

If you were ready to move on, be a grown woman and say, I'm done. Then step out into the lonely world of single uncertainty and look for Mr. "I Want To Spend The Rest Of My Life With You." You didn't do that because you were still giving effort to the relationship you were secretly trying to leave or were you? If things miraculously changed for the better with your old boo, you would have cut off the rebound you were secretly talking to and texting. You would have never mentioned the rebound, hoping your man never found out you were pursuing another relationship. Or, maybe you would have mentioned the rebound and made him seem like a nonchalant, uninteresting date: "Oh, it was just a free meal." I understand why you didn't tell the person you were in a relationship with about the person you met. You had to be sure! You had to be sure you liked him. Plus, it felt good to have new attention, new conversations, and new laughs.

Isn't it so much easier to move on from your past relationship when you are already talking to your new boo? "A bird in the hand is worth two in a bush!" (lol!) You had to be sure you weren't trading something for nothing. What's wrong with that, right? What's wrong with moving on and being happy?

You can't help that you bumped into someone, and after days, weeks, and months of constant contact, you started to like him. Days, weeks, and months you neglected the man you told you loved, the man you told you'd never cheat on him, the man who trusted you wouldn't break his heart and leave him out in the cold. Days, weeks, and months you stopped working on your relationship to secure your rebound relationship. We all know, the rebound has to work! You can't break up and then find out the rebound isn't a slam dunk; you have to score a few goals first.

I know, the relationship was already over. Okay, if the relationship was already over, why didn't you permanently end it? Why were you secretly talking to someone, knowing the person you were in a relationship with had no clue you had moved on? If the relationship was over, why did the rebound know you still had feelings and were dealing with your ex? "Rescue me, O Lord, from liars and from all deceitful people" (Psalms 120:2 NLT).

> *Okay, if the relationship was already over, why didn't you permanently end it?*

Listen, do whatever you feel, but be honest about your actions. If your ex did the same thing you did or has done the same thing you did, I'm sure you didn't like it. I'm pretty sure it hurt you and changed you as a person. If you loved a person and considered him your boyfriend and one day someone called to tell you your boyfriend got married this past weekend, wouldn't that hurt you? Wouldn't you feel betrayed? You'd feel so empty, stupid, and ashamed. You wouldn't want to do that to anyone.

Now, look at you. You're doing the same things men did to hurt you. Remember when your man was talking to other women while you thought you two were happy? When he was going on dates while you thought you two were working on your relationship? When he was texting and laughing on the phone with a new attraction while you were hopelessly waiting on him to call or ask to see you? Now, look at what you've become. You've become like the person who hurt you the most. You can dress it up and explain it however you want to, but you and I both know it's wrong. I don't know if this would be considered the beginning of the ho phase or a ho moment, but it's not the way a queen or a lady would conduct herself. A queen can't choose when to have high standards.

Yeah, I know you both said you were broken up during the time, and things weren't the same. But you and your arena knew you two were still talking, taking trips, and making love between all the bad days. My Grandpop Carlis has been a pimp for over sixty years. Being a pimp, he has so many phrases and sayings, and one of them he says is, "She's my lady and another n***** maybe!" It's true. You all have become just as bad as men, if not worse. The same things that scorned you, you've now become. Everything you used to look down on is now acceptable. I want you to remove the "maybe" my Grandpop Carlis mentioned at the end of his quote and replace it with never.

Many people are cheating, leaving, and ruining relationships behind feelings. It's okay to have feelings, but you need to have a productive, constructive, and open-minded conversation about your thoughts, wants, and feelings with the person you love. If you two can't seem to find a medium, find someone to help you communicate openly and honestly to discover if the relationship is salvageable or not.

As much as we all loved Martin and Gina's relationship on the TV show, *Martin*, even their relationship had its struggles and issues. We have to allow grace back into our relationships. God gives us grace every day. He doesn't make decisions based on feelings. He decides based on facts. Even with all the facts He knows about us, He still grants us grace.

Do you consider yourself someone who is honest? Do you consider yourself as having morals and principles? If you do, you have integrity. If you have integrity, you've never done the things I mentioned in this chapter. If you have done any of the things I've mentioned in this chapter, you need to realign your life

> *Do you consider yourself someone who is honest?*

with integrity. You need to practice integrity in your relationship. If you have integrity, you will always do the right things in your relationship. You will always be gracious, respectful, honest, trustworthy, hardworking, responsible, helpful, virtuous, and patient in your relationship.

Each characteristic will prevent you from ever violating your vow of love to someone. Integrity is a requirement in any relationship that plans to last until death does them part. Each characteristic I mentioned above is an example of integrity. No matter what good or bad feelings you have, you will always do the right thing because you have integrity and you respect the role you play in your relationship. Faith and integrity in your relationship will bring you peace. "Jesus said to the woman, 'Your faith has saved you; go in peace'" (Luke 7:50 NIV).

Things get hard in any relationship. Things get difficult between siblings, parents, cousins, friends, and lovers. I once told a woman she gave the family she rarely saw more grace, loyalty, and love than she gave me, and I was with her every day. Her response was, "Yes! That's my family." She was right. That was her family. We have no choice but to see family at a funeral or family reunion and speak to them no matter how much we do or don't want to. Imagine if no matter how big the indifference you and your significant other have, you had no choice but to see and talk to him for the rest of your life. That's exactly how long God intended intimate relationships to be!

You have to learn and understand that, although your significant other isn't blood-related, he is the closest and most intimate person in your life. You have to allow him the same forgiveness, mercy, grace, and love you may give an absent father, evil brother, jealous sister, or distant cousin. You have to love him with the same, if not more, love and compassion you give those you had no choice of being bound to—family. You chose the person you are bound to in your relationship. The only love you choose in life is the person you marry. Somewhere along the line, you focused more on the way out of the relationship than on how to maintain a long-lasting relationship. You would never do some of the bad things you have done to the person you made love to and loved, to your family. And you may not see or talk to your family for months and sometimes years. You may get upset and mad at your family, but you would never plot, plan, lie, hurt, and conspire to deceive them.

Your relationship and marriage should be more of a deeper connection than any relationship you have or had. To have a thirty-year marriage, you will have to find a better way to manage your feelings. You have to find a way to give the love and grace you give your family to the person you love. Put an end to temporary feelings making permanent decisions in your life. Temporary love seems permanent until your permanent love is gone. Trust me.

I was in Egypt not too long ago and after leaving Jesus's crypt where he lived as a child, we went to the Prophet Muhammad Ali's mosque and tomb. While we were standing in the mosque, my guide, Hamza, shared profound and wise words. He said, "If a woman loves a man, she should love him like her son. If she loves him like her son, she will never stay mad at him. If she loves him like her son, she will never be disloyal to him. If she loves him like her son, she will always take care of his needs and spoil him. If she loves him like her son, she will always love and protect him. If she loves him like her son, she will never do anything that will hurt him. If she loves him like her son, she will always forgive him. If she loves him like her son, even if he loses his way, he will always find his way back to her. If she loves him like her son, he will always love her more than anyone else in the world until the day he dies. If she loves him like her son, she will never abandon him."

Do you love the person in your life the way you would love your son? I realized I wasn't being loved the way a woman would love her son. I realized I wasn't displaying unconditional love to a woman the way I love my daughter. I thought that was so deep! You have to love a man as if he is a part of you. You have to love a man as if you are his rib and you have to love a woman as if you gave her your rib to live. If you love a man as if he is a part of you, you will never think of abandoning or hurting him. You will never run away. If you love and care for him like your son, you will always treat his love with kindness, integrity, mercy, and grace. No matter how he makes you feel, you will always love and forgive him. You will always strive for a happy ending. You will never go out and get another son. "The Lord will create a new thing on earth— the woman will return to the man." (Jeremiah 31:22 NIV).

I was once in a relationship and the woman I was involved with wanted me to do things the way she and her arena wanted. I wanted to do things the way "we" needed. I knew it wasn't about what she wanted or what I wanted. Many of her actions and lack of actions were based on her feelings and those around her. We can all be selfish with our wants. I knew it didn't matter what hurt us or made us unhappy in the past; only the present mattered. Had we decided to move forward together to pursue true happiness, none of our past mistakes mattered. I knew we needed to consistently spend time with each other, correct and learn from our past mistakes, and to be honest about our hopes, desires, wants, and needs.

A fulfilling relationship should be full of the trust and love that two people share, supporting and helping each other achieve their respective wants, dreams, and ambitions.

> *A fulfilling relationship should be full of the trust and love that two people share.*

I knew we needed counseling and someone unbiased to help us get past our past, plan a future, and execute the present. She didn't want that. She wanted what she wanted, the way she wanted it. She "felt" she deserved for things to be her way after all the things I did to her and everything she had been through with me. Maybe she did. I honestly wanted her to have everything she felt she deserved and more. I truly did. I wanted her to be happy. I wanted to make up for all the times the man I used to be made her unhappy. She deserved that. However, I didn't want to sacrifice my happiness to make one person happy. We both needed to be happy and find the ability to communicate effectively, compromise, compromise happily, forgive, heal the past as much as possible, be present for the future, and be willing to grow the relationship. And we needed good counsel to help us attain those goals.

A good counselor would have helped us learn how to communicate better and gain the things we both wanted and needed in our relationship. A good counselor would have helped her deal with any anger, hate, resentment, bitterness, and shame she felt towards herself or felt towards me for the pain I inflicted. A counselor would have helped her forgive herself, and more so, me. Forgiveness doesn't mean she would forget, but a good counselor would have helped her work towards identifying, understanding, and communicating how my injustices affected her life and our relationship. The counselor would have helped us work towards reconciliation and work on letting go of the past. This would have helped her develop positive feelings and decrease any negative emotions she felt towards herself or me.

Maybe this is why Hamza said, "If a woman loves a man, she should love him like her son." Maybe then, forgiving and forgetting the awful things I had done to her would have been an easier thing to do. Forgiveness is a choice. Happiness is a decision. You have to remove the hate from your heart to positively move forward in your life. You can't allow your past to blow up your future. I wanted to heal our past and do what was best for our present and potential future. It didn't work. She wanted to do things the way she felt, and that's okay. She deserved that choice. I hope it led to what was best for both of our futures. I hope the rebound I found out about at the end of our relationship became more than a *slam dunk* and was a game-winning shot. If not, she made the wrong choice based on feelings, and just like you, she will be thinking about the question I asked you at the beginning of this chapter: if your true love shows up on your wedding day and says run away with me, what do you do?

ARE YOU A PATIENT?

*D*o you have solace? I talked to my brother, Marcus, who I call Cash, a couple of days ago. He told me, "B, at this point of your life, you have to do what brings you peace. Whatever that is, I would encourage you to do it and don't expect anything in return, but the solace that you did it. Do it because you know in your heart, it was the right thing to do. After that, let go, and let God."

He wanted me to follow my heart, even if what was in my heart was rejected. He wanted me to be at peace with my decision despite the outcome. True peace is found in one's self long before we can find it in someone else. It took the majority of my life to realize that. I learned, after a lot of lost loves, hurting people I didn't want to hurt, and countless amounts of money spent trying to create happiness, that I had peace inside myself all along.

A lot of you are trying to find wholeness in something or someone else. We've all seen examples of this. Some people display happiness when they get a new job. "I got the job! God is good!" Some people display happiness when they get a new car. "I got a new car! God is good!" Some people display happiness when they enter a new relationship. "Finally! Thank you, Jesus! You finally answered my prayers and sent me someone to make my old boo realize the good thing he has lost! God is good!"

> *A lot of you are trying to find wholeness in something or someone else.*

So, let me get this right. God heard your prayers, got rid of your old boo, gave you a new and better boo, and now God has made your old boo miserable, lonely, and sad? God also made whomever your ex ends up with not as good as you were to him? God also made sure his new boo doesn't look better than you and their sex isn't as good as yours? Ha! Imagine God blessing you by hurting someone else. Nope, it doesn't work that way. Just because you're happy that doesn't mean your former partner has to be unhappy. I get it! Trust me, I've heard so many women say, "I found someone better!" Yes, you may have found someone better for *you*. You should always find someone better. If you're growing in your life and meeting new people with every relationship you have, you should learn something new about yourself. The person you left, or left you, didn't lose the best thing in *his* life. I know it feels good to think he did, and hope he finds no one else like you, but most people do find someone better for *them*. That doesn't make you or him a lessor person. It just means that with each relationship you had, you learned a little bit more about yourself and what you need and will need to be in your next relationship.

Truth is, no one wants to meet another you. If he did, he would have just stayed with you or you would have stayed with him. There are those rare occasions when true loves fall out of love and have to find their way back to each other. Usually, it's after one, if not both, have experienced some new things, grew a little bit more, and then they came back together.

Some of you will praise a new relationship just because it's new. It's no different than someone loving their brand-new Honda better than the Honda they purchased new three years ago. The new Honda is just newer! Three years from now, they'll feel the same way they felt about their old Honda about their new Honda, so calm down. The new Honda may have different features, but nothing stays new and perfect forever. Older people call this the honeymoon phase. I know you want your ex to feel like you found someone better and life's great, but why? Why does it matter? Your ex may care, but eventually, he will move on too. How often have you seen one of your exes promoting their new boo and thought, *Oh, they did so much better than me*? NEVER! (lol!) People hope and pray a person changes, and when they don't, they move on. Guess what comes next? The posts! The "I'm happy!" "God has answered my prayers!" "God is good!" You fly your new boo's flag, but eventually, that flag fades. Your new boo may be great and refreshing, but it's probably because you two don't have a past yet. When you fly that new flag representing your new boo, are you trying to convince everyone else this is the best man for you or are you trying to convince yourself? Are you trying to convince everyone else that your new car or new job is making your life better or are you trying to convince yourself?

Happiness isn't found in a person, place, or thing. Happiness isn't found in a new boo, old boo, or rebound boo. That's why you see people going from person to person, place to place, and thing to thing, repeatedly. Those things only bring people temporary happiness. True happiness has to be found inside yourself. You have to nurture and take care of your happiness throughout your life. If you're relying on someone else to provide you happiness, they'll eventually fail you. And guess what? You'll eventually be looking for something or someone else new to provide you happiness, again.

> **Happiness isn't found in a person, place, or thing.**

Before I get too far, do you remember in Chapter One when I said being happy and being fulfilled are two different things? Let's replace the word "happy" with the word "fulfilled" when it comes to oneself. I'm happy; I have a new mate. I'm happy; I have a new car. I'm happy; I have a new job. Great! You can be temporarily happy with any of those things. However, to be fulfilled inside and out, you must love yourself first, even if you find a job you want for the rest of your life, a car you want for the rest of your life, or a man you want for the rest of your life. If you aren't fulfilled with who you are mentally, physically, emotionally, and spiritually, you will never find solace. You will never find peace. You will never feel completely whole. You will never be satisfied in life. You will always look to outside people and things to make you feel temporarily happy.

Fulfillment isn't found in a person, place, or thing. Fulfillment isn't found in a new boo, old boo, or rebound boo. True fulfillment has to be found inside yourself. Are you fulfilled? If not, you're probably draining a man of his happiness at this very moment. You're probably expecting him to help you find happiness every day. Not that your friend, family, or mate shouldn't make you happy, but it's not their job to be your court jester. God didn't place them in your life to heal all of your brokenness. Have you ever heard the adage: "Hurt people, hurt people"? It's true. The more the person you say you love tries to help you, little by little, he loses himself. Little by little, he becomes more like the person he's

> *True fulfillment has to be found inside yourself.*

trying to help. How? The deeper you've been damaged, the bigger the court jester he has to be. He tries, maybe unsuccessfully, to make you happy every day. That's a tough job to do for anyone.

Your parents created you and they failed at making you happy *every* day. Maybe that's why the Queen in *Alice's Adventures in Wonderland* would constantly tell the court jester, "Off with his head!" Imagine every day you're responsible for someone else's mood. Every day you're responsible for making someone happy who isn't happy with themselves. How can you make someone feel fulfilled who isn't capable of feeling fulfilled with who they are on their own? It's a very tiring job to be someone else's smile. On the days you fail at making the person happy, the person becomes depressed, sad, angry, insecure, and even suicidal. When a man sees the woman he loves depressed, sad, angry, and insecure, he wants to do whatever it takes to make her happy. The woman he loves becomes a patient and he becomes her court jester. He watches the things he does and says around the patient because he doesn't want to upset her. If that doesn't work, he limits his time with the patient to avoid upsetting her. He knows one wrong statement, joke, or lack of action can make the patient angry, enraged, depressed, sad, and insecure. Eventually, the court jester avoids the patient to prevent her from being unhappy.

Do you think this strategy works? No. The court jester, the significant other, has now chosen to be alone instead of taking the chance of upsetting the patient. Inevitably, the court jester's distance only upsets the patient more. The patient doesn't understand why the court jester doesn't want to come around and why the court jester doesn't do things with her. The patient doesn't understand why the court jester acts differently now and why the court jester doesn't talk when they are together. The relationship has turned into an obligation for the court jester. Whatever the court jester's patient is going through, the court jester's life has to stop so he can go through it with her too. If the court jester's patient cannot do something, he can't do it either. If the court jester does it anyway, he doesn't enjoy it because he feels a sense of guilt since his patient cannot enjoy it with him. If the court jester's patient cannot live a normal life, the court jester's way of life becomes abnormal too. Now they both feel trapped.

The court jester has to be mindful of everything he does. Even simple things require cautious judgment and precise decision-making on whether to stay, leave, or speak when in his patient's presence. He feels horrible every time he makes his patient upset. He no longer feels comfortable being himself. The court jester has become broken, angry, sad, depressed, and insecure in the relationship.

Remember I said, "Hurt people, hurt people"? Do you see how one person's brokenness broke their partner? It's not on purpose, and most of the time, neither of them see the destructive pattern happening in their relationship. Don't get me wrong. The broken person, the patient, may try to make the person she's draining happy too. This behavior is usually due to brokenness and insecurities. Those insecurities could

be how she looks, who may look better than her, or if she sat-
isfies her partner the best physically and sexually, compared
to his past partners.

This sexual insecurity usually results from a past relationship she may have been in and was cheated on. She may
feel as though she fell short and subconsciously may blame
herself for the things that happened, even if they weren't her
fault. Now she feels more insecure. Therefore, she goes above
and beyond to prove her loyalty by trying to over-perform
for her new partner physically and sexually.

Most patients in a relationship are overly sexual or great
gift-givers. Both of those things, sexual and material, only
provide momentary happiness. Sex and material things will
never make a person feel fulfilled. Whether you're the giver
or the receiver, you will only find temporary happiness with
sex or gifts. Due to the patient's previous relationships, she
will try to do everything she believes she failed at in past relationships with him. She will do anything she believes will
keep him from cheating or abandoning her like her past partner did. She will do almost anything for her current partner
sexually. If she was physically abusive in past relationships,
she may try not to be physically abusive with him. If she
used to drink a lot of alcohol in past relationships, she may
try not to get drunk around him. If she was promiscuous in
past relationships, she may try not to sleep with someone else
while with him.

Unfortunately, it never goes as planned. Eventually, she'll
get insecure, sad, or angry, and she'll throw something at

him. She may blame him for the things she forgot she did while out drinking with him. Last but not least, she'll exchange numbers with someone during one of their "in a relationship out of a relationship" moments. She may tell him she changed a lot compared to how she was in past relationships, but she didn't.

Truth is, who she was in past relationships is still there, hidden. She's still trying to find out who she is and who she wants to be in a relationship. The drunk wasn't who she was in past relationships. The abuser wasn't who she was in past relationships. The promiscuous person wasn't who she was in past relationships. The behavior she's portrayed in relationships were coping mechanisms for deeper issues she failed to address and heal, issues that alcohol, sex, gifts, time, effort, and loads of reassuring can't heal.

Have you ever seen a relationship where two people couldn't be split apart and they seemed perfect for one another? Fast forward and the relationship is falling apart. Usually, it's because someone has serious inner issues they are refusing to address and get help with. Issues they have been dragging into every relationship like Santa's bag of treats. They're looking to their mate to help them fix it.

> *They're looking to their mate to help them fix it.*

They believe their mate is the answer to their "happiness." They have made the role of their mate so complicated and demanding that their mate feels alone even when they're around. They've become their mate's patient. They've added the role of doctor to their boyfriend or girlfriend. They've turned their mate into a court jester. Have you been turned into a court jester? Can you be happy if you're spending every minute of your life trying to make someone else happy? Every day you're putting your happiness aside to search for a cure for your partner's unhappiness. Guess what? You'll never find the vaccine. They are their own vaccine.

You will only lose yourself trying to find a different treatment to treat them with daily. You may even have affairs to find moments of happiness for yourself. But you'll never find happiness from the affairs. You'll more than likely feel emptier than before and put yourself at risk for more issues. You'll feel worse after cheating because you really want to be at home, happy, in bed with the broken person you love. You're not there because you don't want to do the wrong thing or say the wrong thing to make them unhappy, which will make you unhappy. You may drink more, but that only masks the issues you're trying to avoid thinking about. Furthermore, alcohol usually causes more problems than it solves. Your alcohol consumption may make you violent, have blackouts, or fits of rage from overconsumption. Mix that with your sexual indiscretions and you're bound for destruction. Now you're looking for happiness in things and people because the person you want happiness from cannot give it to you. Do you see it? Do you see how the court jester has become the patient? "Hurt people, hurt people."

Now there are two damaged unhappy people looking for someone else to help them conquer their emotions, past issues, secrets, and demons. The communication, bond, and love have become broken and damaged by inner issues that neither can fix alone. You have two patients looking to each other for the cure, the vaccine, and the remedy. Impossible! If they stay together, they need to find professional relationship help. If they break up, they need to find professional personal help. They need to stay far away from another relationship until they find the help they need to heal and feel self-fulfilled.

This relationship was salvageable at the beginning. The best thing the court jester could have done was support the person he loved while she sought help from a professional for her bad habits and personal issues. While his partner is being helped with her personal issues and healing, they both could have found a good relationship counselor to help them make the correct steps towards a healthy, happy, and fulfilling relationship.

My friends and I know a lot of women who have been molested, assaulted, and raped. Most women we know didn't get help and they didn't tell their parents. Those wounds were brought into every relationship they had. They couldn't see how the deep-rooted issues they had hurt and helped destroy a lot of their relationships. I could see the similarities immediately from one woman to another. They were my girlfriends, but more so my patients. Every day they needed something, and deep down inside, I knew I couldn't give them what they needed. From the bottom of my heart, I wanted to provide them what they needed. They wanted me to fix something they couldn't fix themselves, something most mental health professionals will have a hard time helping them fix. I once heard someone say, "Closure is a myth." I believe that. We grow used to coping with some things in our life, but there's never true closure to some of the devastating events that have happened to us.

Unfortunately, we bring those mental and physical scars and bruises into our relationships. We turn our companion into our doctor, psychologist, and psychiatrist. That's not what a relationship is supposed to be like. For a man, if you're lucky, you become the man the woman you love opens up to. That's a marvelous feeling at the beginning. You both feel more secure because you two have established a huge amount of trust between one another. You have no idea the demons you're about to experience and expose yourself to. You have no idea that some of the demons you're about to be exposed to will grab hold of you and change the very person you are.

> *We turn our companion into our doctor, psychologist, and psychiatrist.*

Looking back, I'm astonished at some of the things I thought were good qualities in women, that were actually consequences of past trauma for them passed off as good qualities. Don't get me wrong, they were good qualities, but they were learned from horrific circumstances. Let me give you some examples of some things women may do in relationships because of things they lack or because they were scarred early in life.

Some women are the epitome of the word "loyal." Have you ever known a woman who dated a man she should have left a thousand times, but she never leaves? Or a woman who has caught her man knee-deep inside another woman, but she's out shopping with him the next day? Or a woman who comes home from work to find everything but the carpet and paint gone because her man gave everything away *again* to the neighborhood corner boy for an eight ball of crack-cocaine, but she's out looking for her man instead of a new place to live until he cleans his life up? I'm sure you know a woman who will let a man hit her, cut her, and smack her in the face, but she won't leave. She will fight you to defend him if you try to stand up to her man. Do you know a woman who stayed with a man she caught cheating while she was pregnant? Do you know a woman who didn't leave a man whom she got arrested with or for, although he left her with the charges?

Before I go any further, I want you all to know I think women are the most disrespected humans next to a Black man. You all are so strong! I long for a day when women are seen as strong for what they have accomplished, rather than seen as strong for the negative things they have absorbed. Okay, let me get back to my point. I gave you those examples of what women go through with men and still find a reason to stay because this comes from abandonment issues. Some people like to call people weak who go through these things and stay, but I will not say that. It stems from something deeper. Some of you are loyal to a fault in your relationships because your father abandoned you. I know countless women who found love in all the wrong places because they were searching for the love, security, affection, care, and protection their fathers were supposed to provide to them all of their life. People call these "daddy issues." Once they find someone who loves them and they love him, no matter what he does to them, they stay. Everyone doesn't deserve your loyalty, sweetheart.

I'm not saying to cheat on him. I'm saying you shouldn't be with him. Your father's abandonment is one huge issue, but the issues you've picked up from your companions who beat you, had babies with other women while dating you, who you've almost went to jail for, these relationships are what cause you to be a patient when you meet a good man. These relationships taught you to drink too much, become physically abusive, and cheat before or after you get cheated on. These are the demons you bring along with you that damage your new love, which turns him into a court jester, then a patient. I understand you want to be a good captain of your ship and go down with it, but it's okay to abandon a ship you're maintaining alone. Go be a good captain for another ship.

I understand your father wasn't around and the guy you were dating became a substitute for your father's absence. He may have taught you about religion, life, drugs, guns, art, money, credit, fashion, or how to start a new business. He may have taken you places, put you through school, helped you buy your first home, made you feel secure and loved. The men you experienced became everything you wanted your father to be in your life, but they always fell short because they could never fill the void your father left in your heart.

Maybe it was because your father was an addict. Maybe your father was a deadbeat dad. Maybe your father died before you met him. Maybe your father was a weekend father who dropped you off at his mother's house on all of his court-mandated weekends. Maybe your father was married to your mother your entire childhood, but never took the time to love, care, and guide you. Maybe he never took the time to tell you about men and teach you how to be a lady. Maybe your mother ran him off because she was bitter he had a new boo and he didn't want to be with her. Maybe your mother had a new boo and didn't want your father around. Maybe you never knew your mother cheated on your father and he left because he wasn't your biological father. Maybe you discovered the man you thought was your father never really was your father. None of these things are reasons to let a man come into your life and hurt you because

> *I understand your father wasn't around and the guy you were dating became a substitute for your father's absence.*

of the things you lacked in a father growing up. None of these things are reasons to lose yourself more than you feel you've already lost.

I know you've had to figure it all out by yourself. I know you've been looking for a man to protect you and keep you safe the way your father never did. I know you've been looking for a man to love you and care for you the way your father never did. I know you're looking for a man to be proud of you the way your father should have been. I know you're looking for a man to tell you how beautiful you are the way your father should've told you all of your life. I know you want a man to tell you, "You is smart. You is kind. You is important." Please allow me to tell you—you are all of those things and more!

> **But you can make a change today.**

I know you can't go back and leave those past relationships. I don't want you to. I know you can't go back and fix what you did in your past relationship that changed the man you used to love. But you can make a change today. God "heals the brokenhearted and binds up their wounds" (Psalms 147:3 NIV).

I don't know if you have issues with your mother, father, uncle, or a family friend. But, today, I want you to seek the help you need to heal the broken parts inside of you. I know it hurts. I know you're in pain. I know some things you did with men were only because you were scared, insecure, and hurt. I know the cry for attention was only because the person you wanted to be there for you wasn't there to give you the attention you deserved and required in your youth. I know you didn't plan to have a baby so young, but you wanted something you could love the way no one loved you. I know you drank to hide the pain from being molested and lacking love. I know you only fought because you had to fight off grown men as a little girl since there was no one there to protect you. I know you only became promiscuous because it was less frightening to give it up willingly than being raped, again.

I know the first heartbreak you ever received was from your father. I know you've been waiting for a man to help you put back together the pieces of your heart that your father broke. You just want to be loved. All your life, you've just wanted to be loved, not for how you look or what you have, but for who you are as a woman, the woman you are on the inside and the outside.

Let's heal the woman inside so she can properly love the woman on the outside. I want you to heal the woman inside, so you can properly love a man and he can properly love the whole you. You've been vulnerable for everyone else you've loved. I want you to be vulnerable with yourself so you can fully love yourself. It doesn't matter how young or old you are. It doesn't matter what you have or haven't done in the past. Today, you will be fully present for yourself, present to accept the things you cannot change and get help for the things you can change. That way you can be happy, have solace, and it won't matter if you're alone or in a relationship.

You will be fulfilled. Always remember to "be thankful in all circumstances, for this is God's will for you who belong to Christ Jesus" (1 Thessalonians 5:18 NLT).

A couple of years back when my daughter was in middle school, I surprised her and took her on a trip to Puerto Rico for spring break. While we were on the plane, we watched this movie named *The Perks of Being a Wallflower*. As we were watching the movie, this kid named Charlie asked his teacher a question. His teacher's response made me say, Wow! I told my daughter what the teacher said is the truth and to never forget it. During the movie, Charlie asked his teacher, "Why do nice people choose the wrong people to date?" and his teacher replied, "We accept the love we think we deserve." I thought that was so deep and so true! Then Charlie asked his teacher, "Can we make them know that they deserve more?" and his teacher replied, "We can try."

That's all I'm telling you to do today. Try. It doesn't matter if you've accepted the love you thought you deserved in the past or you gave someone the type of love you thought he deserved in the past. From today forward, you will start healing so you and the person you love both know you deserve better and more from one another. I want you to fulfill your love as two whole, happy, and fulfilled individuals together. In the words of Jimmy Valvano: "Don't give up. Don't ever give up."

IS YOUR MAN INSECURE?

$\mathcal{W}$ here should I begin on how f**ked up we are as men? Ladies, I salute you for all the bulls**t you take from men. Lord knows we couldn't put up with the things we put you all through. All the countless nights lying awake in bed wondering where we are, who we are with, what the h*ll we are doing, and who are we doing it to. All the times we have called you fat, ugly, stupid, dumb, whore, slut, the B-word, and so many other names your parents didn't give you. We

> **How many times have you caught your man cheating, lying, or misleading you and he's blamed you for his indiscretions?**

use those foul and disrespectful words to deflect from our own failures, setbacks, and downfalls.

How many times have you caught your man cheating, lying, or misleading you and he's blamed you for his indiscretions? How many times has your man lied or ignored the proof you've presented to him about his outside affairs? How long have you been embarrassed to tell someone about the man you love because you fear the things someone may tell you about the man you are deeply in love with? Do you remember the first time you looked in the mirror and doubted yourself because of the things he said or did to you? Do you remember the first time you asked yourself, "I wonder if he was doing these same things to another woman," while you two were having sex?

You used to think he was invincible! You used to think he would never do awful things to you, and even if he did, he would never let it get back to you. You thought he loved you far too much to hurt you. You used to be happy with each other all day, but now you only argue when he's around. You don't want to argue, but anytime you try to talk to him, he resists. You've become this nagging, insecure, and sheltered woman. A woman you said you'd never become. Who are you? Who have you become? How did you lose yourself like this? You're a wonderful woman! Why can't he see it? All you desire is to be happy with him and for him to only want to be happy with you. Why is this so hard? Why is this so difficult? If he loves you the way he says he loves you, this shouldn't be so hard.

I felt I had to speak on this topic because I am a man. And as a man who has done these types of things to women in the past, I know we play a huge part in breaking the women we love down. We break your brains, hearts, and spirits. We spend our entire lives trying to master the game of attracting and sleeping with multiple women. Generation after generation, men teach their sons, nephews, little brothers, cousins, and friends how to get women, manipulate women, sleep with women, and keep the woman they love, all while sleeping with as many other women as possible. Does that sound about right? Did I shock you? I hope I did. This is a real topic of conversation. Ladies, this is for you, but this is also for all the so-called real n*****, hustlers, bosses, pimps, gangsters, and players who felt like Snoop Dogg was speaking directly to them when he said, "We don't love them hos!"

> *Men are taught that women are objects, new toys, and trophies at a very young age.*

Men are taught that women are objects, new toys, and trophies at a very young age. Ladies, you all have to absorb some of the blame for this as well. When you hear your boyfriend, husband, or brother asking your son if he got "some" yet, you don't step in. Most of you ignore the conversation or simply laugh it off. You don't realize you're indirectly aiding the problem instead of stepping in and saying NO! This isn't the proper way to discuss sex, ask your son if he's having sex, or promote sex to your son, nephew, or little brother.

There has been a conversation that men have been having for decades, if not for centuries, with younger men. The conversation always ends with the question, "Have you had sex yet?" That question immediately motivates young boys to have sex with the first girl who will let them have sex with her. That question, most of the time, eliminates the "good girl" who isn't having sex for the girl having sex. Which makes the "good girl" who isn't having sex want to have sex so she will feel more secure and fit in. The "good girl" has no idea she will feel less secure about herself after

> *"What's your body count?"*

the guy she's given herself to sexually moves on to another girl to add more names to his list of sexual partners. I think you call this "bodies!" The continued cycle of boys trying to have sex to prove they're a man, and girls having sex to fit in and feel more secure, has spawned the most popular question today, "What's your body count?" If you haven't been asked that question yet, you probably will be asked at some point in your life. You may even be asked, "What's your head count?" I don't want to know your body count or head count, but there was a time in my life that the answer to that question would determine if, or if not, we would be more than just sexual acquaintances.

Ladies, what flavor chewing gum are you? Are you Hubba Bubba, Bubble Yum, Double Mint, Winter Fresh, Bazooka, Big League, Big Red, Extra, or Juicy Fruit? Why? Because that's what most men treat you like—a piece of gum. Some of you have been chewed so many times that the sweet, juicy, fresh piece of gum you used to be is now dry, tough, chewed up, and tasteless. We are taught as young men you are not a treasure we should, well, treasure. We are taught that you are a piece of gum we can chew, spit out, and get another piece. Sadly, some of you ladies stand by silently while this broken mentality is passed down from one generation of men to another.

> *Ladies, what flavor chewing gum are you?*

This mentality is the reason a lot of men have made you a baby momma. This mentality, along with the direction we receive from the men in our lives we look up to, teaches us that sex comes before love, sex is above love, and it's always about the sex, not the love. This cycle also teaches women that it's okay to be an object, if you're the object a man chooses at the end of the night. Most women don't want a man to cheat, but they accept it because everyone says, "A man is going to be a man," or "That's what men do." You've watched us go from woman to woman for so long that you've blinded yourself into thinking this way of life is normal. Men have to cheat, right? If you're not giving him "some," he has to get it someplace else, right? That's a hoax.

Many people believe men have no self-control. As a former sex addict, I get it. It can control your thoughts and actions occasionally. You may want it as much as you can get it. I'm sure there are severe situations and some people do have serious issues controlling their loins. I don't doubt this. But, if normal people and overly sexual people don't have self-control, how do we go to work, spend time with our kids, watch the game, wash the car, visit family, play sports, and go to jail? I have friends who have served 100 to 240 months in prison and I believe they had self-control during their time in prison. I'm sure most men who are incarcerated have self-control. For most of our lives, we have to have self-control, even if it's involuntary.

Imagine if we were taught to voluntarily have self-control. Paul the Apostle wrote, "But the fruit of the Spirit is love, joy, peace, forbearance, kindness, goodness, faithfulness, gentleness, and self-control" (Galatians 5:22 NIV). This is the way men should *love* a woman. Paul's words are the true definition of how to love a person. Imagine if we were taught that a true relationship and bond are executed by the act of love, joy, peace, forbearance, kindness, goodness, faithfulness, gentleness, and self-control. It would remove any foul act a person could make in a relationship. Imagine if young boys were asked, "Do you know the proper way to date?" instead of "Have you had sex yet?" Imagine if young boys were taught to court and marry a woman, instead of being asked how many bodies do you have? "Encourage the young men to be self-controlled. In everything set them an example by doing what is good" (Titus 2:6-7 NIV). Imagine if a man was taught to treat you like his treasure instead of his favorite flavor of Bubblicious.

Men, we have to discontinue this narrative we are passing down from generation to generation. Ladies, you have to teach little girls to stop being the temporary star of a man's X-rated movie. Men have learned and been allowed to treat women like meaningless objects for so long it seems normal. Over time, we pick up more tools of bad habits that we use to insult, manipulate, use, and abuse the women we love or want to have sex with. Most relationships men have start off in a dysfunctional manner. Women hope their love and loyalty will persuade the man to become different. You hope we see you as more than just sex. You hope we see you are different and better than the rest of the women in our phones and DMs. Most relationships men have with women start with sex. Maybe it's date one or date three, but sex usually enters the equation early in the relationship. There are women I've dated who are probably reading this book right now who just learned my name from the book's cover.

How many men have you had sex with before you knew his first name, last name, age, and birthdate? How many

> *Men, we have to discontinue this narrative we are passing down from generation to generation.*

men have you slept with before you asked him if he's married, single, bi-sexual, or sterile? Ladies, you are taught to
find love and keep love with your body. That's impossible!
This continued way of thinking will, more often than not,
leave you with another body count and no man. I'm sure
you've heard women say, "Men are physical." Yes, most men
are physical. Being physical is in most men's nature, the same
way it's in a dog's nature to bite. You can be a good dog owner
and teach your dog to bite a chew toy, a ball, and his food.
Or you can be a bad dog owner and teach your dog to attack
and bite another dog, person, or even you.

A great deal of men have been teaching little boys the
same way a bad dog owner teaches a dog to be bad. Just
because the dog can bite that
doesn't mean it has to attack
everyone. A good police dog
is taught to attack a crimi-
nal. It can bite anything it
pleases, but with proper
guidance, the dog doesn't.
Men can teach young men to control their behavior, as
well. We can teach our sons, nephews, and little brothers
to respect, care for, love, cherish, and treasure a woman.
"For where your treasure is, there your heart will be also"
(Matthew 6:21 NIV).

> *Men can teach young men to control their behavior, as well.*

We can teach young men to be physical only when it's
to protect the one they love. How do you protect the one
you love? By not harming the one you love. By not only

protecting them from someone else's bad actions and bad words, but also protecting them from our own bad actions and bad words. The bad habits men are taught as young boys ruin us as adults.

As young men, we are taught to sleep with as many women as possible. When we get older, the same women allowing us to sleep around with them, change their tune, and want us to stop sleeping around, settle down, and marry them. So, let's get this right. You all have given us unlimited access to all the theme park rides and now you want us to give all of that up, to ride one ride? Imagine that! That's going to be a tough campaign trail for you to win. We are taught that we can ride any and every ride as many times as we want to for the rest of our life. And you think we will give all of that up to ride one ride? Good luck!

Young men should be taught to observe, study, and learn about the rides they are most interested in. Then they can decide which ride is better suited for them. Once they choose one ride, it should be made known that *then* they can have unlimited access to that one ride for the rest of their life. I guarantee if this mentality is taught to young boys growing up, you'd see far more monogamous men.

Do you remember how excited we were as kids when our mother told us we could have one piece of candy in the store? That one piece of candy made us so happy! I'm sure you remember a time when you came home with a bag full of candy, so excited to have so many choices of sweets, but failing to realize how upset your stomach will be after you ate the entire bag of candy. All I'm trying to say is, sometimes less is more.

The most impactful thing Dr. Hannah told me was, "You don't respect yourself by allowing so many women to have had you!" Fellas, that was the *realest* sh*t I've ever heard! If I'm supposed to be all this and all that, how can I let any and everyone have access? Makes no sense. There should only be one special lady with that type of access. This is the direction we should be giving to young boys and girls. There shouldn't be countless people who can identify the sounds you make during sex. There shouldn't be countless people who know what you look like naked. There shouldn't be countless "bodies" that have been under, on top, in front, and behind your body.

> *"You don't respect yourself by allowing so many women to have had you!"*

Men, we have to teach our legacies better. Ladies, if there's no man around, you have to teach your sons and daughters to be different. "Start children off on the way they should go, and when they are old they will not turn from it" (Proverbs 22:6 NIV). This is true. It won't always go as perfectly as we hope, but it'll be better than leading them the wrong way or not leading them at all.

I think I was five years old when my ten-year-old friend, Brock, persuaded my five-year-old girlfriend, Santrice, and me to do the oochie-coochie. Brock found a cardboard box somewhere around the building and set it up for Santrice and I to go inside the box and hump each other. At five years old, we learned how to have sex from our ten-year-old friend, and at ten years old, he obviously had learned how to have sex from someone else. Around the same time, the older guys and girls had taught and pressured Santrice and me to French kiss in front of the entire project apartments. I remember all the kids and teenagers standing around us as we kissed. But what I remember most is, five-year-olds don't do the best job of brushing their teeth. (lol!) Nonetheless, by the age of five years old, I had already learned that a man lays on top of a woman to have sex and you have to put your tongue in a girl's mouth and her tongue in yours to French kiss. This is a true story.

Isn't it amazing the things men will pressure men and women into doing? Men will also make you feel like what you're doing is the right thing to do, even if it isn't. Uh oh! Here comes the manipulation, peer pressure, reverse psychology, intimidation, and fear we will conveniently use to get what we want. Some men will even use physical force. None of this is okay, but if you're ever the victim of intimidation, fear, or force, please report it to the police. If you don't do it for yourself, do it for the next woman or little girl that man may abuse, rape, or kill.

Okay, I had to share that, but what was I saying? Oh yeah, isn't it crazy that the night before a man's wedding day, our friends, uncles, brothers, and dads are pressuring us to have sex with another woman before we say "I do" to our soon-to-be wife? They will use reverse psychology, manipulation, and peer pressure to influence us to sleep with another woman the night before we get married to the love of our life. Sometimes a man may be fresh out of a stripper's or prostitute's vagina, a vagina making a living all night long having sex with any fat, bald, stank, rich, broke, tall, short, burning, young, old, diseased, circumcised, or uncircumcised man with a couple of coins to pay her with at the end of his turn. Then we hop right out of that used, abused, and spoiled cow and jump straight into our new wife's vagina. Yep! That's how we consummate our marriage, ladies.

The saddest part is most women accept this tradition. Let me get this right: He loves you, proposed to you, is about to marry you because you two want to be with each other faithfully for the rest of your lives, but he has to cheat on you one last time before he says, "I do" because he won't be able to sleep with another woman once he's married to you? Oh, and you're okay with it? Is that really how you pictured Holy Matrimony? This is the way men teach men to step into a lifelong commitment with the woman they love. Not to be biased, because I have seen and heard how crazy and nasty bachelorette parties are too. But right now, I'm talking about my brothers.

From young boys watching cartoons to grown men about to get married, we are teaching each other one thing—have sex with as many women as you can! We aren't teaching each other to be faithful. We aren't teaching each other to have self-worth. We aren't teaching each other self-control. We aren't teaching each other to be loyal. We aren't teaching each other to be with one woman. We aren't teaching each other that women aren't objects. We are teaching each other to have sex with as many women as possible, even on your wedding day, and *don't get caught!* (lol!) It's not funny, but I had to laugh because we are crazy as h*ll!

We would lose our minds if the woman we love had this mentality. A lot of men have lost their minds when the woman they love did the same lying and cheating he's been doing all of his life. Ladies, what is the phrase you all say, "He won't like it if I give him a dose of his own medicine." Let me tell you, he won't! (lol!) I know this because I know I wouldn't like it if any woman I dated did the things I did to her, to me. It's sad and unfair, but it's true.

Let me ask you a question: Is your boyfriend insecure? Look around and make sure the coast is clear before you answer my question. I don't want to cause any issues at home. (lol!) He may never admit it, but deep beneath his ego is a broken, sad, angry, lonely, and flawed man. Dr. Hannah once told me, "Your ego is your imposter. Your ego is made up of all the things you want people to believe about you. Some of those things may be true, but your imposter isn't the real you. You may not even know the real you anymore because you've been living as the imposter for so long. You created the imposter to protect you from being hurt. You created the imposter to be tough, a ladies man, a gangster, a hustler, and this popular

> **"Your ego is your imposter."**

guy everyone wants to be, and all the ladies want. You created the imposter to protect you from being vulnerable and transparent. The imposter is your ego. Everything you let people see—the cars, clothes, penthouse views, and playboy lifestyle—is your imposter."

The Bible says, "For everything in the world—the lust of the flesh, the lust of the eyes, and the pride of life—comes not from the Father but from the world" (1 John 2:16 NIV). She told me I had to be "vulnerable and transparent" with my flaws. She told me, "You have to forgive the people who have hurt you in your life and apologize to the people you've hurt." She told me, "You've allowed the imposter you created to protect yourself, take over your life."

Your imposter is the image you portray to yourself and people. It may be your perfect body, car, clothes, shoes, home, motherhood, fatherhood, or how gangster you are. Your imposter could be who you are at work, in the streets, or who you used to be. Your imposter is your image. A lot of you post and promote your imposter every day on your favorite app. Dr. Hannah also told me, "Your imposter has come into your relationship. The gangster and boss you are in the streets aren't who are supposed to come home to the woman you love. You may have to be that person for those people in the streets or business, but that uniform is supposed to come off when you get home to the lady and family you love."

The imposter is the reason your man feels like he has to impress his friends by sleeping with that prostitute on his lunch break, running a train with his friends on the insecure and possibly suicidal girl in college, get head in the restroom from the girl he just met in the club, and take trips abroad to sleep with pretty Dominican women. The imposter is the pride and ego you can't seem to break through with your man. He may have been feeding his imposter all of his life, like I did.

> **The imposter is the pride and ego you can't seem to break through with your man.**

I was a young big-eared, big-lipped, big-eyed, big-nosed, crooked-smile, skinny, broken, fatherless, latchkey, poor kid from Richmond, Virginia. The older I got, the tougher I got. The more money I made, the better my clothes got. The more dope I sold, the cleaner I kept my Ferrari engine. The more my songs played on the radio across the United States and abroad, the more women I got. The more my name grew in popularity, the more women I entertained. The more alcohol I mixed with my ego, the wilder the sex was. The moment the number one NFL draft pick, Cam Newton, moved in next door to me, the D-Boy who came from nothing and became a notable rapper, you couldn't tell me I wasn't the sh*t. I grew from a boy who never smiled to a man who believed he had an amazing smile.

With every flyer, concert, and party I was paid to perform solo or along with Jeezy, Meek Mill, Lil' Wayne, Rick Ross, J. Cole, D.J. Drama, T.I., Plies, Drumma Boy, Diddy, etcetera, my eyes, nose, and ears seemed smaller. My lips became more sexy than big. Women became trophies. I remember telling a woman she wasn't the catch; I was! My imposter could see no wrong in how I looked, what I did, or what I said to you or the person I loved the most.

I'm sure you know a man who got the job, car, or lifestyle he wanted, and slowly but surely, he felt and acted like Nino Brown, Scarface, The Godfather, and Pablo Escobar. Scarface had a massive ego. Nino Brown disrespected women, friends, family, and the woman he loved. The Godfather was better, smarter, more powerful, and wiser than everyone, but hated. Pablo was a philanthropist one moment and a homicidal sociopathic monster the next. These men loved themselves the most and died behind their own ego, pride, and lack of wisdom. They were too smart for their own good. The smartest move they could have made for themselves would have been to quit while they were ahead.

Sometimes it's hard to look in the mirror and tell yourself it's time for a change. Their selfishness and refusal to change from the person they were cost them everyone and every-thing they loved. Do you know anyone like that? Do you know someone so trapped in his own light he can't see it's only darkness surrounding him? He can't see that his ways are ruining his life? He can't see how lost he is and he won't allow God, or you, to help him find his way back to the person he used to be or should be? The ego, pride, and imposter in our lives prevent us from being who we truly are inside.

Inside, I'm a man who wants an agape love with one woman. I want a woman I'm excited to see every day for the rest of my life. A woman I crave daily. A woman I'm obsessed with spiritually, mentally, emotionally, and physically. Before I started having sex, gaining popularity, and making money, I wanted to fall in love, true love, get married, and have children with my soul mate. I wanted to have what I was deprived of as a child. I wanted to love a woman the way I wanted to see my mother loved by a man. I wanted to love, protect, guide, and reassure my children of themselves and their God-given gifts and talents—the way I wanted to be loved and reassured with confidence by my father as a child.

We create flaws in our children when we don't teach them the correct way a man and woman should behave. We create flaws and opportunities for outside people, TV, and social media to exploit our children's lack of self-esteem because we didn't teach them self-confidence, reassure them, show them love, and teach them self-love. Thus, they grow up insecure and find security with the wrong man or woman, having empty sex and worshipping material things. Ego and pride fool us into believing these things are real and they represent who we are. The more

> *We create flaws in our children when we don't teach them the correct way a man and woman should behave.*

money, cars, clothes, homes, and the better your body looks, the more you believe those broken pieces inside of you are healed. Trust me, none of those things will make you feel better. None of those things heal you either. Instead, the more you gain, the more you lose yourself.

I've been blessed to be in my daughter's entire life. For a lot of those years, I provided money and material things more than my presence. I was there, but I wasn't present. I spoiled her, took her to school, and bought the class cupcakes and Chick-fil-A, but I wasn't present. One day, I realized I wasn't being the father I always promised myself I'd be when I had children. I guess I looked at myself in the mirror. I had given up the streets years prior, but I was still touring and making music. Therefore, I retired from the music industry shortly after I realized that lifestyle was destroying my relationship with the woman I love and the young woman I created. I knew I needed to be there to teach her how to be a young lady, how men think, what they do, and that she has to love herself no matter the cost. I taught her to be strong and to have pride in herself and never allow herself to be manipulated for material things or because she is feeling down or to keep a man in her life. Spending so much time with her, I realized that I was teaching her the right way to be as a woman, but I wasn't being the right man for the right woman I was raising her to be. I had to stop, look in the mirror, and correct that. In the book of Corinthians, Paul says, "When I was a child, I talked like a child, I thought like a child, I reasoned like a child. When I became a man, I put the ways of childhood behind me. For now we see only a reflection as in a mirror" (1 Corinthians 13:11-12 NIV).

I love Paul the Apostle! I love his story. I relate to his story and I'm sure a lot of you can too. Paul was a man walking in darkness, just like you and me. Paul was named Saul until he met Jesus and saw the light. Saul was doing a lot of bad things, including killing and judging people for what he felt they were doing wrong in his eyes. He thought he was doing the right thing for a long time. Saul didn't realize his eyes were wide shut. Then, one day God removed the scales from Saul's eyes and he could finally see what was right and how his past ways were wrong. That's how most of us are living. In our eyes, the way we see it, we are doing the right thing.

There's a statement I read by Helen Keller I felt exemplified the transition in my own life from Saul to Paul. She said, "It is a terrible thing to see and have no vision." That quote touched my soul. For most of my life, I could see, but I had no vision. My ego, pride, and imposter made me believe the foul, disrespectful, selfish, and rude person I was, was okay. I was too blind to see what I was doing wasn't right, and no matter how often the people who loved me told me I was wrong, I could see no wrong in the things I was doing. Thank God for removing the scales from my eyes! God can give you vision, as well. "One thing I do know, that though I was blind, now I see" (John 9:25 ESV).

A man has to be willing to open his eyes, have faith, and believe. Can I ask you a somewhat personal question? Are you dating a drug dealer or a former drug dealer? Is he ego-driven, prideful, selfish, and rude? Is he a liar and manipulator? Would he rather die or go to jail than look weak? Did he seem invincible to you until, one day, you caught him cheating or found out about a secret baby, and at that moment, he wasn't Superman to you anymore? You thought he would never let you down until, one day, he let you down so far that you could never climb back up again. He should have left you long before you finally left him.

> *A man has to be willing to open his eyes, have faith, and believe.*

I want to apologize to you for every smack, punch, b***h, whore, and slut he ever called you. I'm sorry for every time he left you at home crying, worrying, and insecure. I'm sorry for all the pain he inflicted on you because he was trying to hide his own insecurities. I'm sorry for the mental and verbal abuse you've received from men like us. I, myself, have said things in anger I didn't mean and it took me a long time before I realized the bad things a man says can stay in a woman's mind forever. I'm sorry for all the pain and anger taken out on you, which was meant for someone else. It may have been for his mom, dad, friend, other women, his failures, his losses, or his broken heart. His ego wouldn't let him tell you he was weak. You wanted him to know he could share anything with you and you wouldn't share it. You wanted him to know it's nothing he could tell you that could make you go away. Why? Because you loved him like he was your son. You wanted him to know that he may not trust anyone else, but he could trust you. Let me tell you something to ease your soul—he knew he could trust you. He knew he had a good girl and his ways changed her and broke her heart. He couldn't be vulnerable and transparent with you because he couldn't be vulnerable and transparent with himself. My friend, Eb, once told me, "Y'all n***** need rehabilitation from that life!" She was right!

I've watched guys come home from twenty-year jail sentences and go right back to the same life. Even the risk of being caught and going back to jail wasn't enough reason for them to live a regular life. They have to be the guy every woman wants, with all the money, cars, clothes, and popularity. The imposter they've created is the only image they want people to know and see. They'd rather die or go to prison than fall off. The same way a fiend will pawn everything in their life to get high, is the same way a man's imposter will throw away his wife, girlfriend, family, even his kids, to protect and maintain his image. I don't care if a man is still in the streets, out of the streets, or just came home from a ten-year sentence because of the streets. He could be a former drug dealer, ballplayer, or Wall Street broker. I'd bet every shoe in my closet that he's probably created a narcissistic, misogynistic, egomaniac imposter. That mind-set and lifestyle ruin us.

We think we can get any woman we want and every woman wants us. We think we are the most gangsta, best hustling, smartest, wisest, murderous, and richest ladies man on the planet. How do you grow a relationship with someone that engulfed in himself? He can do no wrong in his own eyes. And if he does a wrong, it's only because *someone else* was wrong first. Every conversation you two have somehow becomes about him. Protecting his image is more important than protecting you. If he's rich, he's the worst person to be around because his uninhibited bad habits are at full speed and no one can question him. Why? Because he's rich. If he's broke, he's the worst person to be around because he's miserable, angry, bitter, and blames everyone but himself for his failures. Every gangster movie he watches is about him and his crew. Even if he has fallen off and is no longer "the man," he would prefer to hold on to his old life and reputation than start a new life and reputation. He would prefer to wait on some miracle to happen in his life to put him back on top than to move on and start a new life with you.

I grew up with a guy who fell off a few years ago. He refuses to move on and start a new life. He's broke, lost his girl, and anything else you can imagine, but he's still waiting on his plugs to magically show back up from Mexico and put him back on top. You know why? So he can prove to people who don't care and never cared, that he's still on top. I'm telling you! That lifestyle we live is harder for us to quit than it is for a user to get off heroin. Ego is the worst drug a person can be addicted to.

This makes me think about King David. David in our time would have been the most violent, feared, gangsta, rich, artistic, pop star musician, and ladies man in town. David killed, murdered, had money, committed adultery, had multiple women, and was the top guy in his crew. He was bigger than life! I mean, the guy did kill a ten-foot giant, become king, father the wisest man to walk on earth, oh, and I can't forget to mention, his bloodline led to Jesus Christ. Can you imagine the size of this man's pride and ego? I wonder how bad things had to get for him to write, "Better the little that the righteous have than the wealth of the wicked" (Psalms 37:16 NIV). David was talking about himself and how his road from rags to riches changed him for the worst. Years later, his son, Solomon, who became the wisest and richest man, wrote, "Before destruction the heart of a person is proud, but humility comes before honor" (Proverbs 18:12 NET).

Some of us have to lose it all before we are humbled. Some of us had to lose our lives to be humbled. Solomon was the wisest man on earth, and even his pride and ego blinded him. Some of you are so blinded by what you want, that you can't see past your own two feet. I trafficked drugs for almost twenty years and it didn't dawn on me one time that the risk didn't match the reward. Why? I couldn't see past myself. I couldn't see past my own wants and desires.

If hindsight is 20/20, I wonder how many people went to jail, died, or lost the people they love before they realized, this sh*t isn't worth it? By then, it's too late. You're a day late and a couple hundred thousand dollars short. Since I left the life of sex, drugs, and entertainment, I have achieved and received three degrees in Information Technology. I also did what most former drug dealers do—I got my CDL license. (lol!)

The imposter traits I'm speaking of start early. Growing up, a lot of men aspired to be like Bill and Claire, then Martin and Gina, but somewhere along the line, some of those men became more like the Fresh Prince, and for some of us, Ghost. Some boys meet a girl and fall in love. But some boys get popular, get money, get cars, and meet a lot of girls. These boys realize that the more money and nice things they have, the more girls they get too. Then they realize if they have more money and cars than the other guys, they get the other guys' girls too. Soon they realize that the more money, cars, clothes, and women they have, the more popular they become. Do you see what's happening?

> **The imposter traits I'm speaking of start early.**

The money, cars, clothes, sex, homes, and girls all become objects that feed their *ego*! They take pride in how many objects they can gain. They want to have more of these objects than any other man. These things feed their

insecurities. These things mask their insecurities. These things are gained and used to make them happy because they are insecure about who they truly are. However, none of these things represent who he is or what he is. He may not know who he is because he only pretends to be what everyone wants and expects him to be.

Change is scary. It's easier to continue doing what seems to work, while deep down inside, he's aware there's no happy ending to this lifestyle. No matter how rich, famous, or pretty the woman is, he will never be fulfilled. No matter how many things you gain in life, you can't take a U-Haul with you to heaven.

Future has this record I love called, *My Collection*. And in my past, it was exactly how I felt about women. He said, "Anytime I got you girl, you my possession/ Even if I hit you once, you part of my collection." Once men have attained the cars, clothes, and money we grew up wanting, we collect women. Every woman we add to our collection gives us a different story to tell. Another "I want to sleep with her" goal met. It's an enormous stroke to our egos to feel like we are the best she's ever had, even if we were the worst she's ever had. Oh, and if she has a man or husband, our egos feel even bigger.

I want to apologize to all the women we, as men, have disrespected, led on, and broken your hearts trying to feed our own selfish egos. I want to apologize personally if I've hurt you. I apologize for my rotten mentality. There's no excuse for men's poor behavior. I want you to know I'm working daily to heal.

A lot of men like me are suffering from post-traumatic stress disorder (PTSD) from our upbringing and dangerous lifestyles. We don't mean to damage and hurt the people we love usually, but since we were little boys, we were taught to have sex with girls and how to get girls is by being the best man. The best man we saw wasn't our father, more than likely. And if it was our father, he was selling drugs, making money, driving new cars, womanizing, and in fancy clothes every day. The guys we looked up to, who had the pretty girls, got them because of their popularity. The Notorious B.I.G. said it best, "Either you're slinging crack rock, or you got a wicked jump shot." Those were the guys who had the prettiest girl or girls. The more popular you are and the more money you have, the more women want you and want to sleep with you.

The nice guy finished last. The seat filler never had a seat. From youth, we learn that we have to get a girl and have sex. The more notoriety we have, the better the women we have on our side. This cycle continues from generation to generation, and I believe that we, as men, have the power to change it. Women have the power to force us to change it, even if we don't want to.

Mikeeyah, my dearest friend, asked me a question the other day. She said, "You really think we [women] have the power to change things, huh?" I told her, "Yes. God gave Adam eternal life and dominion over the earth, moon, sun, stars, and every animal, bird, plant, and fish created. Adam traded it all because the woman he was sleeping with asked him to eat a piece of fruit. Adam betrayed God to make the woman in his life happy." Furthermore, Adam sacrificed a part of himself when God took one of his ribs to create Eve. Eve was living proof that women are the most important addition to a man. But, like Eve, women have to be careful how they use their gifts, because women have a sense of power over the things men do and don't do. Every decision and choice we make is in the pursuit and for the attention of a woman. Men wouldn't play sports, shower, work, hustle, rap, or anything else if it didn't ultimately end with a woman's attention.

> **We don't need women to act like men.**

Yet, women have been evolving year after year, becoming more like men. This distorted way of thinking has created more divided and broken families. We don't need women to act like men. It's time to make some grown-up decisions for you, your relationship, and your kids. The man you may be in love with, the man I was, and the man I'm working on daily to change, will never leave you. If you leave, that will be the only time he tells you he misses you. More than likely it's true. He's involuntarily being vulnerable to prevent more damage and hurt to his already damaged and broken heart. There are a few men who will only tell you this because he doesn't want to lose his possession. Sometimes men don't want you; they just don't want anyone else playing with their toy. It'll affect his pride and ego if you leave him. He's the type of guy that even if you move on, he's already moved on a dozen times.

As far as the men who truly miss you when you leave, I apologize. He was never taught to be vulnerable to a woman. He was never taught to be transparent. He was taught to be tough and never get caught! He was taught that if you do get caught, never tell. He was taught to never cry, never say you're scared, and let no one get close enough to hurt him. Some men may be vulnerable with their kids, but it's only because they see themselves in their kids. They want to protect them and be everything to their kids, the way they wanted someone to protect and be everything to them.

You want him to love you the way he loves his kids, but he can't. His kids will always be a part of him, no matter the distance. A man's love for his kids differs from his love for you. You can break his heart and he's already had his heart broken too many times in his life. For most men, it's not *if* you will break your loyalty and trust to him, it's when. Frankly, he wasn't ready for you. He needed to seek a counselor to help him deal with and conquer his demons. I'm not saying he didn't love you; he just loved you the best way he could during that time of his life. He loved you, but he wasn't ready to love you the way you deserve to be loved. How could he love you when he didn't love himself?

> **A lot of men are broken.**

A lot of men are broken. You meet us in a broken state. We have wounds that aren't healed. We aren't prepared to be in a healthy relationship. A lot of women fall in love with our potential to be a good man, good father, and good husband. But, if we are not healed and healthy, it's impossible for us to be the man you want and deserve. It's impossible for us to be the man we deserve to be for ourselves. We have to heal, and after we heal, we can step into a relationship healthy. You can't heal us. We can't heal you. We have to do that on our own timeline and out of our own desire and need. We can support one another in a relationship, but we can't force someone to be healthy enough to participate in a healthy relationship.

Some of you know what I'm telling you is the truth because you're hurt, broken, drained, bitter, and resentful because you tried to force an unhealthy man into a healthy relationship and he wasn't ready, so he never fulfilled your expectations. He never became the man you fantasized about and pictured him to be. He may never be ready. He may be ready after you've broken up and moved on. You may be upset because you went through h*ll with him and now another woman has the man you were supposed to have. Now, all you have are the bad memories.

You have to recognize the healthy and unhealthy traits in the person, or *patient*, you're dating at the beginning of courting him. Address those issues right then without delay. Either the person you're dating is ready to heal and have a "HEALthy" relationship, as Dr. Hannah says, or he is not.

If he is not ready, leave immediately! It doesn't make you or him a bad person. It makes you a mature partner who's honest and using good judgment about what you two need to do to have a healthy relationship. Unhealthy can become healthy together, but it takes *two* willing individuals and possibly good counsel. If you all can't do that, leave. You'll save both of you a lifetime of hurtful and painful memories.

I'm telling you this because I was an unHEALthy man in relationships with HEALthy women. I broke them. I hurt them. Why? Because I wasn't ready to heal or recognize that I needed to heal and put in the required work to be a positive part of a healthy relationship. It's okay to date, but the moment dating becomes courting, and courting becomes a relationship, the relationship should be on a healthy course. Where I am now with my healing, if I was your man, I'd tell you. I'm sorry I didn't walk away before I broke your heart. I didn't want you to walk away because you were like a part of me. I knew there was nothing I could do to make you leave, but shut you out. Unfortunately for me, that's what I did, and for that, I apologize. I'm not asking for absolution, and honestly, I don't deserve it.

That's what a man who's in the process of healing his wounded life would tell you. That's what a man learning to be more vulnerable and transparent would tell you. That's what I'm telling you. This is a man who put his ego and pride aside so he can love you the way you deserve to be loved. This is a man who looked in the mirror and finally saw his imposter and didn't like the way he looked. I created a monster.

But, day by day, I'm killing the Hyde to my Jekyll. I can't wait to see who I am. I can't wait to be who I truly am to the woman I love. I dream of the day, that even if I'm falling, I'm still lifting the woman I love up! Selfless love!

You can do it too, my brother. You need to talk to a professional. You need help healing the pain and hurt you built up inside of you. It's okay. Even Tony Soprano saw a counselor once a week. We have been street soldiers, sergeants, assassins, and generals all of our lives. That's not normal. We've been dealing with trauma from murder, paranoia, broken hearts, kicked doors, broken homes, federal indictments, and broken relationships since we were kids. We've been dealing with depression, sleep deprivation, and anxiety all of our life. You cannot be fully cognizant if you're dealing with so many things mentally. You have to stop tucking the pain away, my brother. There's no more room to hide the pain, hurt and disappointment in your life. The demons inside of us have been running the people we love away. The hurt inside of us has been hurting the people we love the most.

> *The demons inside of us have been running the people we love away.*

I can't lie to you. It's going to be a process. Dubai wasn't built in a day. But trust me, it's doable. I'm living proof! My entire life was darkness. The Bible says, "The people who walk in darkness will see a great light. For those who live in a land of deep darkness, a light will shine" (Isaiah 9:2 NLT). The light had been shining on me for a long time. I finally opened my eyes to see it. Open your eyes, my brothers. It's your choice to stay in the darkness or walk into the light. I loved the streets, money, women, and violence. If we're being honest, I miss the smell of a fresh brick of cocaine every day. (lol!) Don't judge or look down on me, please. It's no different than someone who quit a lifetime of smoking, gave up coffee, or stopped eating sweets, to crave it occasionally. Even when I was making great money in music, I still missed being in the kitchen cutting, blending, weighing, and bagging. It's okay. Our pasts will always be a part of us, but it doesn't have to define our present and future selves.

The Bible is full of stories about people who overcame their past struggles and made it their testimony. "Let the redeemed of the Lord tell their story" (Psalms 107:2 NIV). Your mess is a message for someone. Clean up your mess, my brother. Clean it up for you, your lady, your mother,

> **We have to change our generational curses.**

your family, and for the young men who look up to you. We are more than womanizers and pursuers of material possessions. We are more than manipulators and mental abusers. We are more than our painful past lives we are trying to mask and escape.

We have to change our generational curses. Talk to someone, my brother. It's the best decision I ever made, along with studying God's Word. I didn't want to go into an office or to someone who may know or recognize me, so I found a therapist online to talk to who was on the other side of the country. Get help. I lost a lot of good people in my life and I wasn't present for a lot of great people I should have been present for in my life. I'm still trying to get past the hurt, shame, and disappointment I inflicted on people I love, but it's okay. Without my past, I wouldn't be the person I am today.

God needs us to go through everything we've been through in our lives so He can use us today. Everything you've been through and everything you're going through isn't in vain—it's your testimony. Despite all of King David's mistakes and failures due to his imposter, God still said that David was "a man after my own heart" (Acts 13:22 NIV). God has you exactly where He wants you to be. It's all lessons for His soon-to-come blessings. A man's wrongs do matter. But it's not as important as what he does next. The right actions now, and in the future, are the best apologies you can give someone for your past mistakes. I believe that. Listen, the past has passed, the present is fleeting, and the future isn't promised. Be present, my brother! Live. Learn. Grow. Love! Remember, it's progress over perfection. Don't let your past hinder your future.

You have to *want* to be different and restore what is broken in your life. Be intentional. HEAL! It starts with you! As men and brothers, we have to hold each other accountable and encourage growth and strength. Although we encourage each other to sleep around, hustle, and get money, we should be encouraging family, love, peace at home and in our lives.

There's a quote of mine that I post as a hashtag occasionally that I believe in. I want to see it manifest in people's lives, including my own. The quote is, "Husbands over hustlers. Wives over flips." We need more men to be good fathers and husbands instead of in jail or printed on Rest In Peace t-shirts. We also need more women to be good wives and mothers instead of pieces of gum.

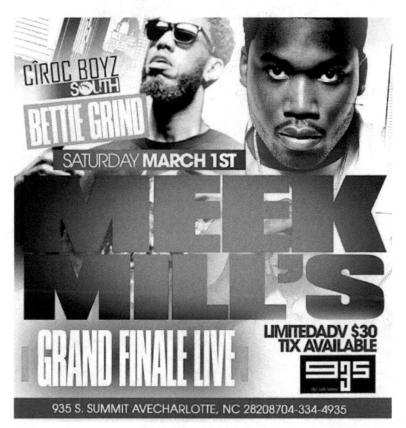

© L.A. Inc. & Adolph R Shiver

© Real Entertainment Promotions & Superhero Ent.

© CBS Radio, WPEG, & Power 98FM

Greg Brown

© Hood Supastar Ent.

MILLION DOLLAR P*SSY?

*H*ave you ever heard the saying: "A man will tell a woman everything he wants in a relationship"? It's true. Trust the words I'm telling you, he will. Will you be listening when he tells you? I don't know. Will you want to hear what he's telling you when he tells you? I don't know. Most men are blunt about what they want from the woman or women they are dealing with. Men, however, don't always know what a woman wants, I'll admit. Maybe that's how shotgun marriages began. A man loves a woman. The same man impregnates a woman. But someone still has to make him marry the

> **"A man will tell a woman everything he wants in a relationship"**

woman he loves, wants, and needs to spend the rest of his life with.

I've watched many fathers, brothers, and male friends tell women that a man knows exactly what he wants. Please tell that to the man who impregnated the love of his life and still had to have a shotgun put to the back of his head to make her his wife. Who knows? The same man with the shotgun to his back is probably telling his now grown-up daughter, "It doesn't take a man that long to know if he wants to spend the rest of his life with you." (lol!) Personally, I don't believe that. Yes, men know the type of car and shoes they want, and the type of women they want to sleep with. It does, however, take some men longer than others to become Mr. "I Want To Spend The Rest Of My Life With You." So, I believe that saying is a lie. Well, I won't say it's a complete lie. We've all toyed with someone else's feelings and emotions, knowing all along, we didn't want them. That's not what I'm saying.

Some men fear being hurt because the relationships they were exposed to growing up were bad relationships. Some men want to be financially secured before they ask a woman for her hand in marriage. Some men want to be able to afford the perfect ring for the woman they love. Some men want to see what qualities a woman possesses before they take the next step. Some men don't want to lose you, but they haven't finished sowing their royal oats. It's true. Sometimes it can be as simple as he doesn't know if she'll say, "Yes!"

Let's be clear. You're daddy's princess. So, daddy will tell his little princess she deserves happiness, love and to move on to a man who knows what he wants. I'm a dad. And I pride myself on giving my daughter unbiased advice. I try to help her see both sides of a relationship. I don't tell her what she wants to hear. I tell her what she needs to hear. If I were like most fathers, I'd probably tell her he's wrong, you're right, and you're too good for him anyway. No, it doesn't take a man that long to know what he wants, but it can if you're not doing the things he's telling you or if he's not doing the things you're telling him. You are telling him, right? You don't expect him to guess or "know" everything he's supposed to be doing, right?

I've heard so many women say, "I shouldn't have to tell a man what to do! He's the man! He should know what to do!" I feel you, but what we don't know, we don't know. I have been in love and lived with women, and I was hurt. So, guess what? I was hesitant to live with another woman again for many years after those experiences. The majority of relationships I witnessed growing up led to divorce, joint custody, and abandoned kids. So I spent the majority of my adult life afraid to fully love, be vulnerable, and be committed to a woman because I've only seen the worst parts of love and commitment. I've never heard my parents say, "I love you" to each other. I don't think I've ever seen them hold hands, kiss, or intimately hug one another.

I had to learn about words of affirmation and quality time from a book. Thank you, God, for inspiring Gary Chapman to write *The 5 Love Languages* because I had no clue that most people's love languages are the things they lacked as a child. Words of affirmation and quality time are things I had to learn and teach myself after failing in relationships with women, time and time again.

I didn't know the proper way to love a woman. I didn't know, and I'm still learning how to properly love a woman. I'm sure a lot of my exes' fathers, friends, and "play brothers" told my exes I should know what to do and I've had enough time to figure out what to do. I didn't. By the way, I don't believe in "play brothers," but I will not get into that right now. (lol!) I'm saying this to say, we all know what we want from our partner and we expect our partner to know everything we want and need from them. But some of our wants and needs have to be expressed even if we think our partner should know. I'm not asking you to express your wants and needs by arguing, bickering, and nitpicking. I'm asking you to express your wants and needs, as honestly and as simply as you would to someone who may not understand how or what to do.

Some of you are talking to your arena instead of the person you need to talk to. You're waiting and waiting and waiting, getting frustrated, instead of just asking, "Hey, do you like me?" or "Do you want me?" or "Will you be mad if I talk to someone else?" or "Do you think I'm wife material?" or "Do you see me as someone you could spend the rest of your life with?" or "Do you want to live with me?" or "I think you are Mr. 'I Want To Spend The Rest Of My Life With You.'" You have to remove the pride from the relationship and be as vulnerable and transparent as you want your partner to be with you.

Every man is different. Most men don't "know" what you want and need to feel secure in a relationship. Sometimes a neutral counsel is needed to help you both get an understanding of what you both expect, want, and need in your relationship. This may be in the present and future. Personally, I've always been the type of man a woman has to ask and be direct with because if you aren't direct and clear with me, you'll never know. I'm hard to read, so you won't know unless you ask. And you'll have to ask in a very gentle and loving way.

> *Most men don't "know" what you want and need to feel secure in a relationship.*

A neutral counsel takes who's right and who's wrong out of the situation. It takes the "I win, you lose" out of the equation. No one feels manipulated, less than, or stupid. There's neutral counsel trying to find a positive way for you both to succeed and win together. This gives you two the opportunity to work out your relationship issues before you two tie the knot. This allows you to let your partner know what you would like to happen in your relationship, in the present and future. It's okay to tell someone you would like to live together someday soon or you'd like to be his wife. Trust me, you'll still be happy when you two find your new home and you'll still be surprised the moment he proposes to you.

I'm not telling you to give him an ultimatum. No one wants to be forced into marriage or kids. I wouldn't want to force someone to do either of those things. None of us are blameless, so we shouldn't be so quick to try, judge, and persecute the people we love. Oneness is far more important than the wedding. Paul the Apostle said, "Then make my joy complete by being like-minded, having the same love, being one in spirit and of one mind" (Philippians 2:2 NIV).

We have to break the curses most of us share, which are we have very selfish points of views. I know you feel like you are the most beautiful and special person he will ever have in his life, but everybody is fungible. My O.G., Pop, once told me, "There's nothing you've loved and lost that you didn't get over." I've listened to men, including myself, talk about how they repeatedly tell a woman what they want from them and some women listen, and some women don't. The don'ts usually come from women who became too comfortable in their relationship or are very independent women.

You know the women I'm talking about. They say, whenever they do fall in love, they will cook, clean, and give their man so much great sex he won't have the desire to go anywhere else but home. But then, somewhere down the line, they lose the desire to do those things. Their man gripes and complains about the lack of home-cooked meals, the dirty house, and most of all, the lack of sexual intimacy. She has her reasons she shouldn't do those things anymore and he has his reasons she should do those things and more. Despite their reasons, good or bad, they become intimately involved enemies who were once head over heels in love with each other. Unfortunately, for them, now they are not.

You know the type of relationship I'm talking about. You might be in one. We all know what usually comes next as their relationship spirals down. The relationship becomes primarily and awkwardly silent, except for the arguments. Occasionally, she may cook, he may clean, and they may step out for a couple's night to celebrate an occasion. The night may end with sex, an "I'm sorry," an "I'll do better," and an "I love you." But after a few days, and no real resolution to fix and mend the situation, things go back to normal—silence and arguments. These arguments usually end with someone saying, "Okay! It can all be my fault! I'm tired of this!" These arguments are usually due to selfishness, miscommunication, a lack of communication, failing to comprehend, a lack of compromise, and most of all, *no couples therapy.*

But today, I'm not talking about cooking, cleaning, arguing and the lack of sex in your bedroom. (lol!) Today, I want to know one thing! How much does it cost? What's your price tag, baby? Are you Forever 21 or are you Neiman Marcus? Are you Longhorn Steakhouse or are you Peter Luger's? Are you in the backseat of a car in a vacant parking lot keeping a lookout or are you The Ritz-Carlton? Are you Myrtle Beach or are you Turks and Caicos? Be careful how you answer those

> ### How much does it cost?

questions because there are no right answers! (lol!) Some of your immediate thoughts were *I'm The Ritz-Carlton! Shiii****! What he talkin' 'bout!* That's cool. I know you've been in a backseat. (lol!)

My daughter, Séyla, told me I needed to write this chapter. She said, "Dad, you have to write a chapter about Million Dollars!" I was surprised! I forgot about the conversation I had with her, but I was beyond proud of her for remembering what I shared with her at such a young age. As a father, you hope and pray you have a bond with your daughter. You look forward to sharing your words, wisdom, and guidance with her. You hope the words, wisdom, and guidance you shared made a lasting impact on your daughter's life. Let me be the first to say, "Thank you, Séyla. I'm elated at this very moment to be writing this chapter you remembered and reminded me I should write!"

When Séyla was a little girl, I asked her these same questions I will ask you in just a few minutes. When I was touring and performing, I was also a motivational speaker for a school program that granted me the honor of visiting schools and speaking to students in inner cities. I was once an inner-city child and I conquered the odds most of those students faced. Despite the odds I faced, I became a successful entertainer in the music industry and a successful businessman. The program coordinators wanted me to tell my story and perhaps it would inspire the students to expect more from themselves in life. Sometimes they would have

Séyla, my greatest love.

Photo Credit: Frank Pitchford @SohoPhotos

me speak to a room full of troubled teenage guys and girls. They would say typical things and ask me typical questions: "Have you met so and so?" or "How much money do you have?" or "I heard your song on the radio" or "Do you have a girlfriend?" or "What kind of car do you drive?" We'd joke and we'd laugh after I answered their questions and then I'd get into my life's journey.

With kids, you have to get their attention quickly and you have to keep their attention the same way you have to with an audience in a sold-out arena. A real arena, not the arena you all keep telling your private business to. (lol!) There's a difference between an auditorium full of inattentive kids and an arena full of fans. The people in the arena know your songs and paid to come see you.

However, in those classrooms and auditoriums, there's no music, they're not excited, and there's no crowd shouting back.

The kids there may not have had breakfast. Their parents may be addicted to drugs. They may be in the same clothes they've worn the past three days. They may have had to borrow a tampon from a teacher. They may be failing school. They may only eat if they come to school. They may be abused, molested, or just buried their best friend. Those 500 sets of eyes and ears were waiting to see how entertaining or boring I would be.

Lord knows being booked to perform at a homecoming full of teenagers would have been far easier, but I wouldn't change those experiences I had with those kids for the world!

I enjoyed them. Some see me out now and say, "Hey! Bettie Grind! You spoke at my school!" Out of all the awards, trophies, and plaques I've received, the award I received for the years I participated in that program and spoke to those kids means the most. Those kids touched my heart! I know my story resonated to them. They opened up and were vulnerable with me because I was transparent and vulnerable with them. I told them I was proud of them because you have to be strong to be vulnerable.

The amazing thing is I didn't realize until this very moment, long before I saw a therapist; I was already being transparent and vulnerable. Maybe it was because I grew up just like a lot of those kids. I came from a single-parent home where some days we didn't have electricity or water. I came from hand-me-downs and food stamps. I came from a home where I witnessed drug addiction. I came from a home where I had to go to school the day after I witnessed the person I love, my dad, being sentenced to ten years in prison. I came from a home where I cried at night because my friends were killed. I came from a home where I witnessed abuse of all kinds on males and females. I did what most kids from that environment grew up to do—sell drugs and carry guns. We hoped we'd make it out of the trap. But, in the back of our minds, we knew we may not live past twenty-one years old.

I told the kids my story and they could see that after all I had been through and faced, it was still possible for them to make it out too. They were fully in tuned. I became a

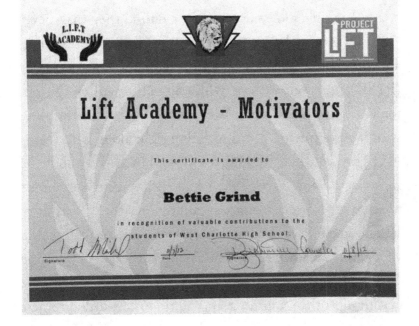

successful rapper with songs playing nationally, driving the hottest cars, mingling with the stars, and living in the best homes money could buy.

We related because we all just wanted to make it out of the struggle and pain. We all hoped one day God would hear our prayers and change our stars for the better. I knew what those kids were going through, whether I experienced it or my friends and family members had experienced it. I could relate. I wasn't someone on TV or online they may never meet. I was with them talking, laughing, listening, inspiring, and motivating. I knew the post-traumatic stress disorder (PTSD) they were dealing with and will be suffering from for years down the road. Why? Because I've been dealing with it all of my life. I was suffering right along with them.

I gave you that backstory so I could tell you about the most memorable experience I had speaking to a group of teenage girls after school one afternoon. Yes, it was after school. I've told no one this story, ever. These young ladies were given a chance to take a class after school to pass to the next grade or graduate high school. These young ladies were getting up in the morning and getting their little brothers and sisters ready for school and to the bus stop before they had to get to school themselves. These young ladies were skipping school to get home in time to get their little brothers and sisters off the bus in the afternoon. These young ladies were selling drugs and some were prostituting themselves to pay for food and shelter. These young ladies were victims of molestation, rape, and abuse. These young ladies were 13-17 years old and some were pregnant.

I still remember their faces. I remember how grown some acted and how timid some were around a strange man. When the teacher and counselor introduced me to the group, only one responded. She was the most *grown-ish* acting, loud-mouthed, littlest, and youngest girl in the room. I remember the quietest and most reserved young lady there telling the youngest one, "Shut up and let the man speak!" The young one immediately sat down. I told them it was okay. She's fine. And I asked the youngest one her name and if she would be my assistant. She agreed. They all rolled their eyes at her simultaneously. (lol!) I made a joke about all of their rolled eyes, and they laughed. Then I talked to the class. It took a little longer than usual, but after about ten minutes of asking them their names, ambitions, and goals, they were all talking, asking questions, and laughing.

The most reserved girl laughed, but she was the last one to talk. She asked me a question about my daughter and how I felt having her young and unplanned. She asked me a lot of questions after I mentioned the age my mother was when I was born and how old I was when my daughter was born. I didn't know where the conversation was going, but I kept peeling back layers of my life because it helped her open up to me, the group, and her teacher and counselor. She told me how she looked down on herself and I told her she was a beautiful young lady, and I could tell she was strong. She told me how the kids in school talked about her and picked on her, so she didn't like to come to school. I said, "I see! You tried to leave five minutes after I started speaking." (lol!) They all laughed and she smiled so big! I forgot to mention that part of the story; I'm sorry. At the beginning of our engagement that afternoon, she tried to leave and her counselor told her, "If you leave one minute early, you will not get credit and you will not graduate." Okay, let me get back to the story.

So, she's telling me how she feels, looks, and why she acts how she acts. She told me about how she's been fighting a lot of the girls because their boyfriends like her or want to sleep with her, and in her neighborhood, the older guys try to sleep with her too. As I'm listening, she asked me, "What do you tell your daughter about boys and sex, and what do you tell her to do?" I immediately applauded her and had the class applaud her for sharing her thoughts and feelings. She was the quietest and most reserved girl there. For her to speak and trust me with such personal things, I was beyond honored. Can you imagine how boring I thought I was when she tried to leave when I started speaking to the class? (lol!) Did I mention she was in her third trimester of pregnancy in high school? I'm pretty sure you didn't picture the quietest and most reserved young lady there being pregnant, did you?

Yes, that's why she was being picked on. That's why the girls in school were threatened by her and trying to fight her. The boys in school wanted her instead of them because she was having sex. She was ditching school so she wouldn't have to fight anyone so close to her delivery date. That's also why so many older guys were trying to talk to her. During the most emotional time of her life, she was dealing with so much turmoil and shame. She was already feeling insecure and uncertain. Then she told me she had no friends. By the time it was all over, I asked the young ladies in attendance to hug her. They all promised to be her friend. They told me they will not let anyone talk about her again.

The counselor and teacher were beyond elated at the conclusion. They said they had never seen her talk so much. But, before this, I answered her question: "What do you tell your daughter about boys and sex, and what do you tell her to do?" Before I started, I said, "It doesn't matter what you've already done. It only matters what you do now." I told her, "This is what I told my daughter. I'm going to ask the entire group, including your teacher and counselor, a series of questions."

> *If you had a million dollars, would you give it to the first person you met?*

Question 1: If you had a million dollars, would you give it to the first person you met? They all replied, "No."

Question 2: If you knew the person for one week, would you give them your million dollars? They said, "No."

Question 3: If you knew them for three months, would you give them your million dollars? They said, "No."

Question 4: If you knew them for six months, would you give them a little bit of your million dollars? They said, "No."

Question 5: If you knew them for a year, you'd give them a little something, right? They laughed and said, "Maybe one hundred dollars!"

Question 6: After two years and you all know each other a lot better, and you're closer, maybe you've been on some trips, and they've met your family, would you give them your million dollars? They said, "No. I might take them shopping and give them a couple thousand, but that's my million dollars!"

Then I said, "Well, if you wouldn't give them your million dollars after one week, one year, or two years, why would you give away the most sacred and priceless part of your body to someone you've only known for an hour, a day, a month or a year? You said you might give them a couple thousand after a couple of years. So, why would you give away your entire body in a day or a couple of weeks? You'll give away something you can never get back and something they will have of yours forever, but you won't give them your million dollars. You can possibly get the money back. But you can never get back the part of you that you gave to him or them, ever."

> *So, why would you give away your entire body in a day or a couple of weeks?*

All of the young ladies, including the teacher and counselor, said, "OH!!!!!"

I said, "Aren't you worth more than a million dollars?"

They all said, "YES!"

I said, "Well, act like it! Say no. If you had a million dollars, you wouldn't give it away. So, it should be harder for you to give yourself away. It should be far harder for someone to have had you."

The young lady who was reserved said, "I'm going to tell him that tomorrow! You can't have my Million Dollars!" They all laughed, and the teacher said, "I have to use that!"

"Flee from sexual immorality. All other sins a person commits are outside the body, but whoever sins sexually, sins against their own body" (1 Corinthians 6:18 NIV).

I asked my daughter those same questions when she told me about the first boy she liked. I asked her those questions to help her see she was priceless and to take pride in herself. I knew little about the Bible back then, but I knew a lot of the women I knew, and some I dated, hadn't been taught or talked to about self-control, self-worth, and self-love by their fathers. My daughter wasn't sexually active, but I wanted her to know how much she was worth *before* someone else tried to convince her that she, or it, was nothing special. I want every young girl and woman reading this chapter to know everything about you is special. Everything about you is priceless. Don't you ever forget it!

Listen, I know I'd be a fool to think those young ladies waited until they were married to have sex. What I do hope is that my words that day might've reached one young lady and slowed her down. Maybe, one did wait until her wedding night.

Nowadays, we give ourselves away faster than we will let someone borrow our car or a pair of shoes. If it takes a lifetime to learn yourself, how long do you think it'll take to learn someone else? Time is God's grace and gift to us. Take your time and get to know a person, *the engine.* If he doesn't want to stick around, it may hurt, but not as much as it will hurt if you give him your body and he walks out of your life.

> *I want a woman to read this book and change her life.*

I want a woman to read this book and change her life. I want her to know it's okay to be different. If one woman reads this book and it changes her path, my job is done.

We all walk through life failing forward. Your failures are tools that teach you how to succeed. You don't have to rush love. You don't have to rush a relationship because your egg life is dwindling. You don't have to rush into a relationship because you want a husband and a baby. We all have it planned out in our heads, but life doesn't come with an instruction manual. We rush to love through sex, and sometime later on in the relationship, you find yourself unmotivated to participate in the relationship. Why? Because, over time, you realize the person you're with isn't the person for you. That's why the women who used to say, "Whenever I do fall in love, I'm going to cook, clean, and give my man so much great sex, he won't have the desire to go anywhere else but home," don't feel that way anymore. Why did their lifelong ambition change? How did they get here? They probably gave someone their Million Dollars too soon, and before they knew it, they were in lust, not love.

You've been looking for love to find happiness, but your happiness is already here. You have to find the light of happiness inside of yourself instead of looking for it in someone else. Self-love is one of the hardest loves to give. Self-love is a gift to yourself that you should open up every day and smile. Control your Million Dollars and be patient. You can't rush what God is growing. Love is a choice. Change is a process. Your tree is still deeply rooted, sweetheart. Your new leaves will grow. Give God time to wither those old leaves away to make room for what's going to be new and beautiful in your life. He will continue to water you until your new leaves spring to life, if you let Him. I can't wait to see how beautiful and strong you'll be with your new self-care, self-love, and His nurturing hand. God pours into you, then you pour into yourself, then you can pour into someone else, and then he can pour back into you. Eventually, you'll be pouring into each other, together. "They are like trees planted along the riverbank, bearing fruit each season. Their leaves never wither, and they prosper in all they do" (Psalms 1:3 NLT).

> *Self-love is one of the hardest loves to give.*

God isn't just getting you ready for something. God is getting that something ready for you, too! Ask yourself a few questions before you allow someone to become a part of your life or remain a part of your life. Is this the person you want to love? Is this the love you want to feel? Does this love nurture you, inspire you, and challenge you? Does this love help you heal and grow? Can this person see you? Seriously, can this person truly see you? Do you trust him with your truths, flaws, and secrets? Most importantly, are you better with him or alone?

> *Quit letting men grab the chalk and put another line up on the chalkboard that represents you.*

There are so many questions you should ask yourself before you invest your Million Dollars into someone. Your Million Dollars should be your investment, not his withdrawal. Don't you want a real man who won't break, fold, bend, or shake? Don't you want a man who won't let up or give up? Don't you want a man who will make it happen by choice or by force? Don't you want a man consistent in loving you?

Quit letting men grab the chalk and put another line up on the chalkboard that represents you. Slow down, hit the brake. I promise it won't hurt as much as those constant letdowns and heartbreaks you have to heal from after you give away your investment. You are an investment and he should be too. If he isn't, leave. You don't have to announce your exit nor do you owe him a reason. That's a courtesy. People do the stupidest things to avoid being lonely even though those stupid decisions still leave them lonely. It's okay to be alone. Peace is priceless.

There are two types of wisdom. The first type of wisdom is the wisdom we learn from someone else's good and bad decisions. The second type of wisdom is the wisdom we learn from our own good and bad decisions. Unfortunately, some of you aren't applying the wisdom you learned from your past relationships to your next relationship. Learning from those failed relationships will help you be more successful in your present or future relationship. You can't continue doing the same thing over and over, expecting different results. You can't continue giving away your body every time you like someone. Are you the whole cow or the milk? You can't continue going through life hoping lustful relationships evolve into loving relationships. Relationships are garments or body parts. Garments are temporary and body parts are permanent. If we lose a body part, we will miss it forever. But, if you lose a garment, you'll eventually get over it and get something new.

A true relationship of any kind should be as important as the bones in your body. A true loving relationship should be as important and irreplaceable as your beating heart. Are you the woman you said you'd be in a relationship when you were younger? Are you the reason you don't have the things in a relationship you would want? Yeah, you could have, maybe, gotten a baby or an engagement ring from anyone. But, are you being the woman you need to be to get those things from the man you want to say you love and want to spend the rest of your life with? These are real questions that deserve real answers.

We all repeat the same cycles that failed us before. We think it's our ex or our partner who is the issue. But truthfully, it's your own flaws and hidden agendas that doom the relationship. Usually, you know what you are stepping into in most relationships. You even expect the lying and cheating, unfortunately. The vow for better or for worse isn't honored very much these days. I recently heard of a wedding where the bride asked the pastor could she say, "For better or for better?" And guess what she said to the groom? "For better or for better." They're good people and a great couple. I didn't attend the wedding, but I did ask about it and the bride's request to change the vows was one of the most memorable moments about the wedding that could be recalled. I'm sure the bride and groom know they shocked or gave a giggle to everyone who attended their wedding and those who heard about it. I wasn't shocked, but it did make me giggle. (lol!)

We are drawn to what our flesh desires or what our spirit desires. One of them causes continued regret and one of them will bring you true spiritual fulfillment. I was watching this movie, *The Gentlemen*, on a flight back from Austria. In the movie, this guy named Mickey said, "I think we all would appreciate living life and feeling love a lot more serious if we realized we are slowly dying every day God wakes us up." Isn't that the truth!

Today is the last day of your life… so far. What are you going to do with it? You would respect your heart, mind, body, spirit, and your relationship a lot more if you embraced those very words Mickey said—living life and feeling love. It seems hard, but it's very simple. BE INTENTIONAL WITH YOUR LOVE.

DO YOU HAVE A
JANKY LOCK?

*H*ow many frogs have you kissed? You have to kiss a few frogs before you find the real thing, right? So again, how many frogs have you kissed? Have you kissed so many frogs that you believe, maybe it's not the frog, maybe it's you? Never in a million years did you think you'd have to kiss so many frogs or that you'd still be kissing frogs at this stage of your life. May I ask you a personal question? How used is your lock? Is it loose? Is it broken? Does it need to be tightened?

One day when we were chillin' Uptown Charlotte at my condo. I told my daughter and my niece, Arianna,

> **"You don't want to have a janky lock."**

"You don't want to have a janky lock." They both looked at me crazy and said, "What?" I repeated, "You don't want to have a janky lock." They were young, so I used Jesus's style of teaching with them. If you don't know, Jesus spoke in parables. They were too young for me to speak to them as direct as I do now. I asked them if they could use different shaped keys to open the door to their house. They both said, "No." I told them they were special locks and many men will try to use their keys to open their locks, but they can't let them. I said a key that can open every lock is called a master key, but a lock that opens for every key is called a janky lock.

> **A lock that opens for every key is called a janky lock.**

They were still a little confused, so I told them only one key is made perfectly for their lock. I said, "A man who has a key that works for every lock will be told he has a master key. But a woman who has a lock that opens for every key will be told she has a janky lock." They both died laughing! They finally got what I was saying. I told them I know it isn't fair, but women don't get the same praise men get for kissing a lot of frogs and they don't get the same reputation men get for unlocking every "lock" with their "key."

So again, may I ask you, "Do you have a janky lock?" I know it's none of my business what you've done or haven't done in the past. You're right. I'm personally only concerned about your present and future actions. But I will be talking about some things in this chapter you may or may not have done, been, or are. I have this phrase I use when I have conversations with women who ask me for dating advice. I tell them, "Control your p*ssy!" Sounds easy, right? How many of you have lost control of your p*ssy after a night out with the girls and you messed around and called Tyrone? You know Tyrone. Lame-a** Tyrone you swore you were done with. You know Tyrone. Tired-a** Tyrone you blocked on your phone, Facebook, Instagram, and WhatsApp. You know Tyrone. Cheap-a** Tyrone who had you get all dressed up and took you to get some d*mn chicken wings at a bar. You know, little d*ck Tyrone, got-a-roommate-at thirty-five Tyrone, stank-breath Tyrone, baby-mama-drama Tyrone, still-live-at-home-with-his-mama Tyrone, can't-stay-out of jail Tyrone, slept-with-your-home-girl Tyrone, you-think-he-might-like-men-too Tyrone. Bad-credit Tyrone. Big-d*ck-but-don't-know-how-to-use-it Tyrone. Great sex, but for every d*mn body! You know Tyrone. I know you know Tyrone, girl! You went out last night, got drunk, and couldn't control your box, so you called his lying a**. You know Tyrone. I'm sick of being lonely, so let me call this n**** over with his trifling a** because I can't control my p*ssy, Tyrone.

How many Tyrones have gotten you to kiss their frog because you couldn't control your flower? How many Tyrones have opened your janky-a** lock? I'll wait. (lol!)

I remember a time when women were the only ones saying, "He for everybody!" Now men are saying, "She for everybody." The roles between men and women have changed tremendously over the years. Women are acting like men. I read a meme the other day that said, "I've never seen a generation of women so proud to be hos, side b*****s, cheaters, prostitutes, strippers, and thots… Sh*t's depressing!" I agree. We are in a time where it is hard to distinguish between the good girls and the bad girls. I sympathize with you good girls. I really do! But, good girls, you all need to police your own. We're in a time where everyone is twerking. Everyone is a model, and everyone is about their money.

I remember a time when being a stripper was a discrete profession. I remember a time when you would see a young lady leave her house at night fully dressed, with a rolling suitcase, and get in her car and go to work at the strip club. Most of her neighbors thought she was a flight attendant or leaving for a trip. Nowadays, strippers and social media models are as popular as professional athletes. Strippers and social media models are now truly "influencers." Our daughters, nieces, girlfriends, and wives are all "influenced" by the women they are watching online and on television daily. I can't forget to mention, once Beyoncé said she was "on that Demon Time," you all took it literally. (lol!) I remember a time when people were afraid to ask for your number or to ask you out on a date through a Direct Message on Twitter because the person they asked might screenshot the message and post it.

In this day and time, OnlyFans is cool! It's cool to be a prostitute. Some women live by what I like to call "The Prostitute Rule"—you want to be treated with dinner, money, trips, and clothes, and in exchange, we eventually get a thrilling night of sex. Men step out and solicit the woman who catches their eye and interests them the most. Women only accept an offer from the man who seems to be the most beneficial to them. Men will wine and dine you until they have spent enough time or money to sample your glass of milk. Women will allow, man after man, to trick on them hoping one day they meet a man who possesses everything they've dreamed of in a man. Women desire a man who doesn't care about their past indiscretions. They hope to fall in love like in the movie *Pretty Woman*. Why do you think so many women love that movie? They relate!

Think about what most women wear every day and what prostitutes who walk the strip wear every day. They are both wearing the same thing. A prostitute's daily uniform is long hair, multiple wigs, colorful wigs, spandex pants, spandex skirt, spandex mini dress, six-inch heels, full make-up, fishnets, and she is looking for a man with money. Sound familiar? They dress this way to stand out and differentiate themselves from the good girls.

Do you have a "Pretty Woman" mentality?

Are you a "Pretty Woman"? Do you have a "Pretty Woman" mentality? Do you get dressed up to go out hoping to meet a man or a man with money? Does a man have to take you out to eat or do something for you before you will give him some nookie?

Other women have what I like to call "Orphan Annie" mentality. What is the "Orphan Annie" mentality? A woman with the "Orphan Annie" mentality is a woman waiting on Daddy Warbucks to come and change her life in an instance. You want a man to drive you around in a nice car, buy you a nice home, furniture, bags, shoes, clothes, trips, and dogs. You want to be "kept." You want him to make sure your hair is done, nails are manicured, and your toes have a full set. You want everything your favorite celebrity, YouTuber, influencer, or Instagram model has. I can't forget the surgeries. You want your butt, thighs, waist, back, lips, teeth, nose, and breasts nipped and tucked by a surgeon in Florida, Texas, or South America. The surgeries you're electing to have only tell a man he can't make you happy. If God gave you the unique and beautiful features you're changing because you're unhappy with His creation, how can a mere man possibly make you happy if God can't?

Is there a surgery that can fix "broke brains"? Yes, a lot of you are suffering from a "broke brain." You can attain and acquire those physical things and you still won't be fixed. You still won't be healed or *whole*. Why? Because your brain will still be broken. Nothing you add, adjust, or remove on the outside of your body will fix what's

> *Yes, a lot of you are suffering from a "broke brain."*

broken on the inside. Honestly, do you possess *all* the qualities of a woman you want your son to aspire for and desire in a relationship? Are you the type of woman you want your daughter to be? Are you the type of woman you want your son to bring home to Momma?

I know, you're the best woman a man could have and your coochie squirts out gold glitter! Lord knows you cannot tell a woman with her own car, home, job, credit, who doesn't *need* a man, that her coochie isn't the best a man ever had. You're right. It is until he lays down beside the next janky lock and chews and spits out her tired piece of gum.

How many of you gave a portion of your Million Dollars to a man because you were lonely, drunk, wanted a new pair of shoes, needed your rent paid, wanted to go on a trip, trying to get over Tyrone, felt insecure, or simply because you couldn't control your lady garden? You don't have to tell me, but you know the answer.

Some of you found Daddy Warbucks and he changed your life. Some of you met Daddy Warbucks and all he wanted you to do is sit there and be cute and mute. Is this really the type of relationship you grew up wanting? Do you just want to be pretty dummies? All you have are your posts of Birkin bags, Cartier bracelets, island trips, and maybe an engagement ring. Some of you are more excited about the Likes you get from the engagement ring than the guy who gave it to you. Although, we've never seen you post a picture of Daddy Warbucks. Unsurprisingly, I used to be that guy. I'd post everything *but* the woman I was dating or loved. And the woman I was dating or loved didn't post me. Not that she didn't want to, but we all know a woman who wants to post her man, but she's scared of what dirty secrets about him she may find out.

Why didn't I post the woman I was dating or loved? For exactly the reasons you think the man you're dating or love doesn't post you. Well, some reasons you may assume, but sometimes men don't want to be posted because we know the woman we're dating has a janky lock and she couldn't control her cootie-cat in the past. Let's be honest, some of you didn't have a Million Dollars when we met you. Honestly, some of you didn't have thirty thousand dollars when we met you. (lol!) Some of you are unhappy, serial dating, and have lost total control of your vajayjay. A lot of you won't date a man who has what you have to offer to a relationship. Some of you won't date a man who isn't on your level, but most of our lives, men have dated women who weren't on our level. Some of you may be dating a guy in a different city, hoping your long distant relationship grows into him wanting to move to your city or him asking you to move to his. But more times than none, he won't move. If you try to force yourself into his home and into his city, you'll probably find out there's another janky lock like you already there. Long distant relationships rarely work. Relationships that live only miles apart struggle and have issues, so imagine the level of commitment and trust a long-distanced relationship requires.

> *I know you're tired of kissing frogs.*

I know you're tired of kissing frogs. I know you're tired of trying different keys. I know you feel defeated. I know you're tired of being a throwaway. How often have you been thrown away after you couldn't control your kitty? How often have you been flipped? Do you know where the term "flipped" comes from? Flipped means you've been flipped over from your stomach to your back by multiple partners. How many men have flipped you because you couldn't control your vagina? Don't answer that question. Change the answer. My brother, Ryan, who I call, Fresh, once told me, "B, their p*ssy belongs to them. They just say it's ours. They're going to give it to whomever they want to have it. They control their p*ssy, not us!"

I'm writing this book because I love women. I want to help women. Please don't displace my words as a form of misogyny or male chauvinism. I want to see a day when a woman calls herself a queen because she's the true definition of what a queen is. Is it worth kissing all of those frogs to hopefully, one day, fall in love with an athlete, business owner, rapper, or hustler? Will the infidelity, insecurity, sadness, pain, and broken heart be worth giving away your Million Dollars? Is it really happiness if you're only living to look down on all the other Orphan Annie's who haven't made it yet? Have you made it or are you living a lie? Are you truly a queen if you had to kiss every frog in the kingdom to finally become a queen? Will the kingdom respect you as a queen? Will your king have the pride in his queen he should have? "Her husband can trust her, and she will greatly enrich his life." (Proverbs 31:11 NLT). Have you taken the time to ask yourself what your expectations of a man are in a relationship? If you did, you wouldn't kiss so many frogs while pursuing your prince.

My close friend, Daniel, or as I call him, D. A., was on Facetime with me the other night. We were sipping, toasting, and talking, and he said, "A lot of us have issues B', but we hide it. No one knows what we are being tormented with in our minds and spirits. People are quick to criticize and offer their negative opinions on someone else's shortcomings because their flaws are hidden. But when their own flaws become public information and they can't hide it, they don't like to receive the same medicine they've dispensed." There's a quote I say, "Be careful who you talk about, judge, and laugh at because if the tables turn, it ain't no fun when the rabbit has the gun!"

> *You have the power to deposit a Million Dollars into yourself today.*

You don't have to remain in brokenness. You don't have to remain in shame. You don't have to remain wounded. Keep moving forward in obedience until you reach your glory. When you reach your glory, show up as your authentic self! You have the power to deposit a Million Dollars into yourself today. Yesterday is gone. What you did in the past was a lesson for today. You cannot correct the wrong choices you made yesterday, but you can start over and make the correct choices in your life today. "Though your sins are like scarlet, they shall be as white as snow" (Isaiah 1:18 NIV).

People may try to heckle you, remind you, and talk about you, but stay on your stage. Don't get off your stage for anyone. You're the star. People will try to pull you off your stage and back into the madness, lessons, and mistakes of your past. Don't allow it. That was just a page in your book, maybe a chapter.

We learn our biggest lessons during or after our greatest struggles. Pray without ceasing! Give God praise through-out every circumstance, because it's His grace and mercy that brings you through your darkest days. It's His grace and mercy that hands you your blessings. Everything you've been through has made you wiser. Nothing is accidental or coincidental. Everyone and everything in your life are for a purpose.

D. A. told me, "The only way to truly understand for-giveness and love is if you are accepted for your good and bad, your strength and weaknesses. Who wouldn't love a person if all they had to judge them by were the good deeds they've done? I need to know the good and bad to love you for you. It's easy to love, like, and accept someone who's only shown you their good and has kept their bad choices, flaws, and mistakes hidden. To truly forgive someone is to treat that person as though they have done no wrong. Love keeps no record of wrongdoings. You haven't truly forgiven someone if you continue to bring it up."

Maybe you need this lesson to truly forgive someone or to be transparent about who you are. I want you to forgive yourself and move forward. You've probably had your character assassinated. Some of you had to do some things you will never tell anyone you had to do. Your invisible wounds are still bleeding. But only you need to remember your past so you don't repeat it. Remember, there is nothing God can't deliver you from. Nothing!

The next time you meet someone you think you may like, ask yourself, is this person serving me? I'm not saying, will he serve you on hand and foot or with material things. Is he serving your mind, heart, and spirit? Is he serving you by helping, supporting, and bonding with you in your mission in life? If not, don't kiss that frog. Is he making you a better person spiritually? If not, throw that janky key away and keep it away from your new lock. Let it go.

> *The next time you meet someone you think you may like, ask yourself, is this person serving me?*

Ragab, my driver, told me, "If you lose it, it's not yours. Let it go. Move on. Don't hold on. You live long by letting go. Maybe someone else will find it and it'll help them." Let someone else find his master key. Maybe someone else will be worth a Million Dollars to him. Life is far more than sexual and material pleasure. You are trying to fill a hole up in your life with things that fall apart and break. Million Dollars equals honoring yourself. It's that simple. Don't give away your honor. Stay solid. Remember, you're solid until you're not. It's easy to remain solid when it's lobster, steak, and Barbados.

But, when life seems to fall apart, and temptation is at its best, will you break, bend, or remain solid?

Solomon said, "He who finds a wife finds what is good" (Proverbs 18:22 NIV). Are you good? Do you want to be found? Are you running? If you are, stop. It's time to face your demons. But don't step to your demons without going to God first. Pray for Him to guide your steps and help you fight your demons. Sometimes you misplace your power and have to seek God to find your strength. Your power isn't meant to hurt, use, and abuse people. Your power, influence, and position should help people. I want to help you. I extended grace and when I needed the same grace back, it wasn't extended. It's okay. I did the right thing. Your blessing may not come from the people you helped or forgave. Don't let people turn you into something you're not. Don't let the demons of your past control your present.

Today truly is a present. Your curses can become a part of your purpose. Your past lifestyle didn't serve you. It only leads to baby mama issues, baby daddy issues, divorce, abuse, cheating, lies, betrayal, and far worse. You can change. God's forgiveness is an undeniable power of God's love and grace. God knows your name and every detail of your story, and He forgave your debt! He knows the secrets you have and haven't told Him and He doesn't remind you of your past. He doesn't abandon you because of the person you used to be. No one knows how far you've come, and no one knows what you've been through to get here.

No one knew I had been homeless, a sex addict, a mental abuser, a deliverer of genocide, a manipulator, a liar, and so much more. God forgave me long before I made a change. He forgave me before I forgave myself. In Luke 17:14 (NIV), He says, "And as they went, they were cleansed." Pastor Casey Kimbrough once said, "He didn't say after they made it there, they were cleansed, or after they did this or that, they would be cleansed. He says, as you start to make your journey in the right direction, you will be cleansed. That's all God's grace and mercy. You don't have to wait to heal to be obedient. Be obedient until you heal."

I understand how you go through things, and then you mess up the things in front of you because of the things behind you. Don't be ashamed of your story. Embrace it. Use it. Make a testimony of it. I did a lot right, but I also did a lot wrong. But I don't regret my road because it led me to God and to becoming a better man. Don't regret the road you once chose. They may judge you, but I won't. "All of us, like sheep, have strayed away. We have left God's paths to follow our own. Yet the Lord laid on him the sins of us all" (Isaiah 53:6 NLT).

We've all had to make a U-turn in life. After David committed adultery with Bathsheba, he confessed to God and said, "Have mercy on me, O God, according to your unfailing love; according to your great compassion blot out my transgressions. Wash

> *We've all had to make a U-turn in life.*

away all my iniquity and cleanse me from my sin" (Psalms 51:1-2 NIV). He also said, "The sacrifice you desire is a broken spirit. You will not reject a broken and repentant heart, O God" (Psalms 51:17 NLT). This is a lesson and a blessing in your life. You have the choice to look at your past as a curse or a series of shameful mistakes, but it wasn't either. Your past shaped, colored, and cut your diamond and made you unique and brighter. You have to believe that. You have the choice to look at the moon's light or the darkness surrounding it. Your story can keep you in darkness or be the reason you see the light. If you're not growing, then you're dying. Growth comes with time. You are allotted time through God's grace. One day, hopefully soon, you'll look back and see how far you've come and how much you've grown.

A couple of years ago, I wrote something that Fantasia Barrino read and reposted on her Instagram page and my words went viral. I was humbled that something I wrote resonated and touched so many people. Thank you for being a vessel, Derickus. "DUB C!" The post I wrote said, "A lot of people, both men and women are mistaking companionships for relationships. The want for feeling wanted for the moment has replaced the need for finding The One and growing together for a lifetime. For instance, a rose we enjoy for a short period of time. It makes us feel happy, special, or secure for that moment. Then it's over, and we are back looking for the next special thing or person to fill that void. But a plant we must nurture, love, talk to, re-soil, re-pot, nurse, water, give light, give warmth, give care, and life to for what could be a lifetime. The water we waste watering multiple roses, we could be using to maintain one plant that could grow with us forever. We need to get back to planting a seed with one person. Helping each other grow. Giving each other life. Even if your green plant starts to yellow or wither over time, or appear to be dying, with time, care, and love, you can give that relationship life again. If you ask an older couple, they'll tell you love takes work. It's not just a feeling. It's not always easy. It's a decision."

Grow your plant until it becomes a tree and then love that tree as hard as an Australian Buloke. In the words of Boaz, "May you be blessed by the Lord, my daughter. You have made this last kindness greater than the first in that you have not gone after young men, whether poor or rich. And now, my daughter, do not fear. I will do for you all that you ask, for all my fellow townsmen know that you are a worthy woman" (Ruth 3:10-11 ESV). Boaz was right. You are worthy beloved. So, despite how grandiose a man may be, always remember these four words . . . LOVE *is the* AGENDA!

Scripture References

Chapter 1

Chapter 2

Chapter 3

Special Acknowledgments

Momma,

You were the first woman who loved me and the first woman I loved. Without you, I wouldn't know love exists. Thank you for loving me with an agape love. Now, because of you, that's the only love I'll accept from a woman. You are my heart. – B.J.

Séyla,

Love is such a small word to use to define how much you mean to me. You taught me a new way to love. You taught me to love selflessly. My words will always be with you, but most of all, my heart and spirit will always be a part of you. You are my best friend. "I love you thiiiiiisssssss much!" No man will ever love you like I do, but marry the man who tries to. – Dad

Mikeeyah,

Thank you for accepting all of me. You've supported me wholeheartedly throughout the process of God realigning my life. You've never treated me differently, and for that, I'm beyond grateful. I remember one afternoon you asked me, "Do you love me, Bettie?" I didn't respond, but I never forgot your question. Yes, I love you. I love you far more than you can ever imagine. Thank you. – Bettie

Greg is an International Transparency Life Coach who coaches singles and couples into becoming more transparent and vulnerable in their relationships. To inquire about booking Greg Brown for a speaking engagement, life coaching, or couples coaching, please contact his management at GregIsSpeaking@gmail.com.

 @GregIsSpeaking

 @BettieGrind

 Bettie Grind